ISBN 978-0-260-60116-2
PIBN 10958811

THE AMERICAS

UNITED STATES TARIFF COMMISSION

THE FOREIGN TRADE OF LATIN AMERICA

A report on the Trade of Latin America
with Special Reference to Trade
with the United States

Under the General Provisions of Section 332
Part II, Title III, Tariff Act of 1930

In three Parts

PART I

TRADE OF LATIN AMERICA WITH THE WORLD AND WITH THE UNITED STATES

Washington
1940

UNITED STATES TARIFF COMMISSION

Address All Communications

United States Tariff Commission

Washington, D. C.

ACKNOWLEDGMENT

The Tariff Commission makes grateful acknowledgment of the assistance received in the preparation of this report from the Pan American Union, and the Department of Commerce, especially the Division of Regional Information, and the Division of Finance which prepared the tables on balance of payments.

In the preparation of this report the Commission had the services of Allyn C. Loosley, Philip Mullenbach, and Frank A. Waring, and others of the Commission's staff. The statistics were compiled by the Statistical Division of the Commission, and the commodity summaries in part III were prepared by the Commodity Divisions.

Scope of the report.

This report examines, for the decade 1929-38, the trade of the 20
Latin American countries with the world and with the United States.
It is divided into three parts; part I deals with the trade of Latin
America as a whole, part II with the trade of individual Latin American
countries, and part III. with Latin American export commodities.   Part
I contains a short description of the Latin American area, a consider-
ation of the commercial policies of the Latin American countries, an
examination of the total trade of Latin America with the world and with
the United States, and an analysis of special problems in the foreign·
trade of Latin America, including those arising out of the present
European war.   Part II, consisting of 20 sections, is a survey of the
commercial policy and the foreign trade of each of the 20 Latin American republics, with special emphasis on the trend, composition, and
destination of exports, and the trend, composition, and sources of imports.   In addition, each section contains an analysis of the trade
of the United States with the particular country.   Part III deals
individually with approximately 30 selected Latin American export commodities, 'for each of which there is a discussion of production, exports, trade barriers, competitive conditions, and the effects of the
European war.

Trade statistics of Latin America.

Because of certain characteristics inherent in the trade statistics of the Latin American countries, they should be accepted with

reservations and interpreted with caution. Especially is this true
when the trade statistics of the various countries are combined to
record Latin American trade as a whole, or the trade of a particular
region of Latin America.

Not only do the export and import valuation systems of the several
Latin American countries differ one from another, but in any one country they may be subject to frequent changes. A few countries employ
the f.o.b. basis for valuations, and others the c.i.f. basis. In
some countries declared values are accepted; in others the valuations
are established on the basis of "official" unit values. An outstanding example of such valuation is that of Venezuelan exports.
Exports of petroleum - the dominant Venezuelan export commodity - are
assigned an official unit valuation, but such exports are actually
worth only about 60 percent of the published values. Another example
is the Guatemalan method of determining the value of imports. To
the declared foreign values there is added 25 percent, an amount estimated to cover the charges for freight, insurance, commissions, and
other charges.

Classifications employed in the export and import schedules of
the trade statistics of several of the Latin American countries are
changed frequently, making comparison of data for some commodities
over a period of years extremely difficult. The import classifications
of Bolivia, Brazil, Uruguay, Venezuela, and Mexico underwent such far-
reaching changes in the decade 1929-38 that it was not practicable to
reduce the statistics (shown in part II) for the earlier years to
comparability with the later years. In the import tables for these

countries in part II, therefore, some or all of the data for the years
prior to 1933 have been omitted.

The various currencies in use in the Latin American countries, and
the different rates at which some of them have depreciated, make the
trade statistics of many of the Latin American countries only approximate measures of their trade.   Some of the currencies, notably those
which are pegged to the United States dollar, are fairly stable; others
fluctuate widely.   The difficulty of converting statistics recorded
in such currencies to United States dollars is complicated by the
existence of multiple exchange rates, and by the allocation of exchange for particular countries or commodities at varying rates.   In
converting the currency of Argentina, for example, it was necessary to
adjust the conversion factors, inasmuch as exchange in the period 1936-
38 was obtainable partly on the basis of the official rate, and partly
on the basis of the free market rate.   In several cases the exchange
conversion rates employed in this report, though proper for converting
import and export statistics, are not even approximately appropriate
for measuring the dollar equivalent of prices in the countries concerned.   The official rate of the Chilean peso, for example, is about
$0.05, and the export draft rate about $0.04, but trade statistics are
recorded in pesos of 6 pence gold.   This gold peso, which is equivalent to $0.2061, should be used only for the purpose of converting
the trade statistics.

The trade channels of certain countries - especially Paraguay
and Uruguay - are such that it is not possible to determine accurately
the countries of destination for exports and the countries of origin

for imports. Exports from Paraguay, for instance, are in large part shipped to Argentina "in transit," and even those listed as direct exports to Argentina may subsequently be reexported from that country as Argentine products. Similarly, Paraguay's imports come largely from Argentina and probably includes many products reexported from that country. The Costa Rican trade statistics do not list imports of commodities by countries of origin.

Certain types of data which would be useful in an analysis of the trade of certain of the Latin American countries are not available. Price and quantum indexes of exports, for instance, are obtainable only for Argentina, Chile, and Uruguay. For the analyses of certain countries, the exports of which consist of one or a few staple products, reliance may be placed on quantity figures and average yearly prices of the leading exports. For countries in which exports are more diversified - for example, Mexico - such statistics are unsatisfactory. Except for Argentina and Chile, price and quantum indexes of imports are not available.

CONTENTS

PART I

TRADE OF LATIN AMERICA WITH THE WORLD AND WITH THE UNITED STATES

ix

CONTENTS - Continued

Appendix

PART I

TRADE OF LATIN AMERICA WITH THE WORLD AND
WITH THE UNITED STATES

LATIN AMERICA - A DESCRIPTION

The term "Latin America" as generally used means that area in the
Western Hemisphere lying south of the Rio Grande. For the purpose
of this report the term is restricted to the 20 independent nations in
that area.[1] These countries may be grouped in four geographic
regions - South America, Central America, Mexico, and the West Indies.

Area and climate.

The total area of the 20 Latin American republics is approximately 8,008,000 square miles. Of this total, 6,952,000 square miles,
or 13 percent of the land surface of the world, are in South America,
218,000 square miles are in Central America, 764,000 square miles in
Mexico, and 74,000 square miles in the West Indies. The area of
South America is about two and one-third times that of continental
United States; and Brazil, which is approximately 300,000 square
miles larger than continental United States, occupies nearly one-half
of the South American continent. The area of the six republics of
Central America is but slightly larger than the combined area of

---

[1] These republics are as follows: South America - Argentina,
Bolivia, Brazil, Chile, Colombia, Ecuador, Paraguay, Peru, Uruguay, and
Venezuela; Central America - Costa Rica, El Salvador, Guatemala,
Honduras, Nicaragua, and Panama; Mexico; West Indies - Cuba, the
Dominican Republic, and Haiti. Possessions of European countries in
Latin America are not included in this report; among these are British
Guiana, Surinam, French Guiana, British Honduras, Jamaica, Trinidad,
and the Netherlands West Indies. Of the total imports of the United
States in 1939 from all countries of the Western Hemisphere which lie
south of the United States, imports from the 20 Latin American countries constituted nearly 95 percent; approximately two-thirds of the
remainder came from the Netherlands West Indies. Exports to the 20
Latin American countries constitute a similarly large percentage of
the total export trade of the United States with those countries of
the Western Hemisphere which lie south of the Rio Grande.

Illinois, Indiana, Ohio, Michigan, and Wisconsin. Mexico occupies an area larger than that of Texas, Arizona, New Mexico, California, and Oregon combined. The three West Indian republics, Cuba, Haiti, and the Dominican Republic, have a combined area roughly equivalent to that of Nebraska.

With the exception of the southern third of South America, most of Latin America falls within an area which is tropical, but for a number of reasons other than latitude the region has a variety of climates. South America extends southward more than 1,000 miles closer to the South Pole than does Africa and is the only southern continent that projects far into the temperate zone. It is not, however, as close to the South Pole as are North America, Europe, or Asia to the North Pole, and, therefore, the temperate portions are not subject to the extremes of climate that characterize similar areas in the northern continents. Moreover, the configuration of the South American continent is such that the broadest section is at the equator. Approximately two-thirds of the continent thus falls in the tropics, and South America has the largest continental area in the world that is truly tropical.

Ocean currents, prevailing winds, and the Andes - one of the world's greatest mountain ranges - exercise a profound influence on the climate of various sections of South America. Although many of the South American countries are completely within the tropical zone, large portions of their areas lie at considerable elevations, and these are subject to temperate climates. In that part of the continent which is in the south temperate zone, the seasons are reversed from those in the United States.

The climate of Central America is determined largely by the mountain and plateau highland and by the prevailing winds. The cordillers the slopes of which are heavily forested, is closer to the Pacific coast than to the Caribbean, giving the eastern section a wider coastal plain. In the coastal plains, the climate is hot and humid; the rainfall is very heavy, and the vegetation luxuriant. In the interior the climate is more agreeable than on the coast, while in the highlands it is mild. Rainfall in most of the Central American countries is well-distributed throughout the year.

Because of the extensive area covered by Mexico, its climate is one of the most varied within a single national boundary. In general, there are two seasons, the rainy and the dry, but the amount of rainfall varies considerably with the altitude and the latitude. In the tropical coastal plains, and in adjacent regions with altitudes approaching 3,000 feet, the climate is generally hot and humid, and the rainfall is heavy. The plateau region of central Mexico, which comprises about three-fourths of the area and includes elevations up to 6,000 feet, is temperate in climate. Here there is less rain; in the valley of Mexico rainfall averages about 25 inches a year.

In the republics of the West Indies, situated in the tropics, the extreme temperatures to be expected in this latitude are modified to some extent by the northeasterly trade winds and by the sea breezes. Here, also, elevation is a factor determining the climate, which ranges from tropical and subtropical to temperate. For the region as a whole, the rainfall averages about 60 inches annually.

Natural resources.

Minerals. - Latin America has important mineral resources, but the
location of the deposits, transportation difficulties, and the lack of
capital have retarded their development. Deposits of copper, tin,
lead, zinc, manganese, and the precious metals, especially silver, however, have been worked extensively. Of the mineral resources regarded
as basic to modern industry - coal, iron, and petroleum - only petroleum has been developed to a significant extent. Argentina, Bolivia,
Brazil, Chile, Colombia, and Peru possess deposits of coal, but South
America ranks last among the continents in coal production. Iron is
to be found in most of the Latin American countries, but the deposits
have remained largely undeveloped. Countries with the principal iron
deposits are Brazil, Cuba, Chile, Peru, and Venezuela. Although in
some of these countries the deposits consist of high-grade ore, their
inaccessibility, the lack of adequate transportation facilities, and
the absence of conveniently located coal deposits have operated to
retard the production of iron. South America is one of the major
world sources of petroleum, with deposits in Argentina, Bolivia,
Colombia, Ecuador, Peru, and Venezuela. Venezuela, Colombia, and
Peru are the major producers, the foreign trade of Venezuela being
largely dependent upon its oil resources.

South America has some of the most extensive commercially available copper deposits in the world. Some copper is found in nearly
all of the countries, but the most important deposits are in Bolivia,
Chile, Ecuador, and Peru. Bolivia contains one of the richest known
copper regions, and Chile possesses extensive reserves, including what

is believed to be the world's largest single copper deposit; in
actual production of copper, Chile ranks second (United States first)
among the countries of the world.   Bolivia is the second largest producer of tin.   Other metals found in South America include lead, zinc,
mercury, chromium, manganese, bismuth, antimony, wolfram, and gold and
silver.   Less important mineral resources in South America include
cobalt, molybdenum, mica, sulphur, potassic salts, lime, marble, agate,
onyx, and opal.

For some materials South America is the sole, or one of the few,
sources of world supply.   Chile is the only country in the world
where deposits of nitrate are known to exist in sufficient quantities
for profitable exploitation, but the commercial production of synthetic
nitrates in recent years has reduced the strategic importance of the
Chilean deposits.   Bolivia is one of the few major sources of tin in
the world, as is Colombia of platinum; Brazil contains what are probably the world's largest manganese deposits.   Peru is the leading
producer of bismuth and vanadium.   Venezuela and the island of
Trinidad contain the world's most extensive deposits of asphalt, and
Peru and Chile are important suppliers of guano.

Mexico has long been an important mineral-producing area.   It
has produced more silver than any other country in the world, and also
ranks as one of the great suppliers of petroleum.   Although silver,
gold, lead, copper, and petroleum are the most important minerals in
the Mexican economy, that country has substantial deposits of other
minerals, including iron, tin, zinc, mercury, antimony, molybdenum,
arsenic, graphite, and cadmium.

Forest resources. - Because of the abundance and wide dispersion of softwoods throughout the world, the Latin American production of woods for export is virtually confined to cabinet woods. The forest resources of South America, however, are extensive and it is not possible here to do more than indicate some of the main products. In Venezuela alone, it is estimated that there are over 600 species of wood. South American forests contain hardwoods such as mahogany, rosewood, ebony, cedar, walnut, oak, and cypress, and softwoods such as pine, larch, poplar, eucalyptus, laurel, and balsam wood. They also contain a wide range of medicinal plants. Other forest products include rubber, coconuts, Brazil nuts, tonka beans, balata, and quebracho and a number of other tanning materials and dyewoods.

Most of the woods mentioned, especially the hardwoods, are also found in Central America and Mexico, and to a lesser extent in the West Indian republics.

Agriculture. - South America produces a wide variety of agricultural products. In its tropical and subtropical areas important crops include coffee, sugar, tobacco, cotton, rice, cacao, bananas, olives, peanuts, tropical fruits and vegetables, citrus fruits, grapes, ginger and other spices, castor beans, tagua and babassu nuts, sisal, and yerba mate. In the more temperate regions and at the higher altitudes in the tropical areas, characteristic crops are wheat, corn, potatoes, alfalfa, flaxseed, and a wide range of other cereals, fruits, and vegetables. Many of these products are also grown in Central America. In that region bananas and chicle are especially important export commodities. Practically all of the commonly known fruits and

vegetables are grown in Mexico; the chief tropical commodities include
such products as sugar cane, coffee, rice, henequen, bananas, coconuts,
cacao, pineapples, and numerous spices.   In the West Indian republics,
the most important agricultural products are sugar, tobacco, coffee,
cacao, bananas, coconuts, cotton, and henequen. •

<u>Livestock</u>. - Appropriate climate, abundance of grazing lands, and
ample vegetation make large areas in Latin America suitable for the
raising of livestock.   Cattle are raised in most parts of the area,
but Argentina, Brazil, Uruguay, and Paraguay have become the principal
producers.   Sheep raising is particularly important in Uruguay and in
Argentina.   Hogs are raised in practically all parts of Latin America.
The stock raising potentialities of Latin America have not yet been
fully realized.   Large areas, many of which are still not easily
accessible, would be available should economic conditions justify their
utilization.

<u>Population</u>.

Population censuses are infrequent in many of the Latin American
countries, the practical difficulties of enumeration being very great.
Consequently, available statistics are largely estimates.   The population of the 20 Latin American republics, at the end of 1937, was
estimated to be 123 million (see table 1).[1]   Of this total, 88,250,000
were in South America, 7,125,000 in Central America, 19,150,000 in
Mexico, and 8,500,000 in the West Indies.   Brazil alone accounts for
approximately one-third of the total population of Latin America and

---

[1] Statistical Year Book of the League of Nations, 1937-38.   All
statistics of population here given are the latest available estimates.

for nearly one-half the population of South America.   With 15 percent
of the land surface of the world, the 20 Latin American republics have
but 6 percent of its population.   South America, with 13 percent of
the land surface of the world, has but 4 percent of the total world
population.

The 20 Latin American countries have an average of 15 inhabitants
to the square mile as compared with 41 for the continental United
States.[1]   In Latin American countries, as in many other countries,
the inhabitants are concentrated in small areas.   Although the population density for South America as a whole is only 13 inhabitants to
the square mile, about three-fourths of the inhabitants live in about
one-fourth of the total South American area.   Vast tracts in the
Amazon Basin and in Patagonia have a population of not more than 2
persons to the square mile.   The population density of Brazil is 13
inhabitants to the square mile, but three-fourths of Brazil's population of 42 millions is concentrated in an area within 100 miles of
the seacoast.   For Central America, as a whole, there are approximately
33 inhabitants per square mile; El Salvador, however, has a concen-
tration of 127.   Mexico has a population density of about 25 inhabitants to the square mile.   In the West Indian area, Haiti, with approximately 255 inhabitants to the square mile, and Cuba with 90, are the
most densely populated.

---

[1] Population density for the 20 Latin American republics is based
on estimates of population as of Dec. 31, 1936, contained in the Statistical Year Book of the League of Nations, 1937-38.   Population
density of the United States was obtained from the Census of 1930.

Table 1. - Latin America: Area, population, and density of population

Country	Area in square miles	Latest census			Latest estimates		
		Date	Population		Date	Population	Inhabitants per square mile
South America:							
Argentina	1,079,965	1914	7,885,000		1937	12,762,000	11.8
Bolivia	506,792	1900	1,816,000		1936	3,000,000	5.9
Brazil	3,275,510	1920	30,636,000		1936	42,395,000	12.9
Chile	296,717	1930	4,288,000		1937	4,597,000	15.5
Colombia	448,794	1928	7,851,000		1938 1/	9,033,000	20.1
Ecuador	275,936	-	-		1936 1/	3,000,000	10.9
Paraguay	2/ 161,647	1899	656,000		1936	950,000	5.9
Peru	482,133	1876	2,699,000		1936	7,000,000	14.5
Uruguay	72,153	1908	1,043,000		1937	2,093,000	29.0
Venezuela	352,051	1936	3,428,000		1936	3,428,000	9.7
Total, South America	6,951,698					88,258,000	12.7
Central America:							
Costa Rica	23,000	1927	472,000		1937	607,000	26.4
El Salvador	13,176	1930	1,438,000		1937	1,665,000	126.8
Guatemala	45,452	1921	2,005,000		1937 1/	2,466,000	54.3
Honduras	44,275	1930	854,000		1936	1,000,000	22.6
Nicaragua	60,000	1920	638,000		1936 1/	850,000	14.2
Panama	32,380	1930	467,000		1936	535,000	16.5
Total, Central America	218,283					7,123,000	32.6
Mexico	763,944	1930	16,553,000		1937	19,154,000	25.1
West Indies:							
Cuba	44,164	1931	3,962,000		1936	4,370,000	98.9
Dominican Republic	19,332	1935	1,480,000		1936	1,520,000	78.6
Haiti	10,204	1918	1,631,000		1936 1/	2,600,000	254.8
Total, West Indies	73,700					8,490,000	115.2
Total, 20 Latin American countries	8,007,625					123,025,000	15.4

1/ Uncertain or conjectural.
2/ Including the Chaco region, of about 100,000 square miles, ownership of which is disputed with Bolivia.

Source: Compiled from Statistical Year Book of the League of Nations, 1937-38, and Statesman's Year Book, 1938.

Latin American countries are predominantly rural; yet they contain one of the great and important urban regions of the world, the southern Brazil-Rio de la Plata area. In Latin America there are four cities with a population of more than 1,000,000[1] and four with 500,000 to 1,000,000.[2] In the 100,000 to 500,000 group, there are about 40 cities. Most of these are located in South America. Central America has only three cities with a population of over 100,000. Mexico has one city with more than 1,000,000 population, and four cities in the 100,000 to 500,000 group. The West Indian republics have only one city in the 500,000 to 1,000,000 group, and four cities in the 100,000 to 500,000 group.

Latin American economy.

Agricultural and forest industries.[3] - The basic economy of Latin America is agricultural and in some parts pastoral. It is estimated that over two-thirds of the population is engaged in agricultural (including pastoral) pursuits. In many of the Latin American countries a large part of this agricultural population operates on a basis of practically self-sufficient family units. Many of the products grown do not enter into international trade, and only to a minor extent into trade within the countries. As far as the principal food products (both vegetable and animal) are concerned, Latin America considered as a whole, is practically self-sufficient. Except for inter-Latin American trade in foodstuffs, rice is one of the few staple food products imported in substantial quantities.

[1] Buenos Aires, Rio de Janeiro, Mexico City, and Sao Paulo.
[2] Santiago de Chile, Montevideo, Habana, and Rosario.
[3] See section on pastoral products for discussion of such products as fresh, frozen, chilled, and canned meats; wool; hides and skins; tallow, and other animal products.

In Latin America, however, a number of agricultural products, and many forest products, are produced partially or principally for export to world markets. The importance of Latin America's agricultural products in the world economy may be gaged by the fact that it accounts for nine-tenths of the international trade in coffee, one-half of the trade in flaxseed, one-third in cane sugar, one-third in cacao, and one-third in castor seeds. In addition, Latin America produces and exports large quantities of cotton, wheat, corn, tobacco, chicle, henequen, tropical fruits, spices, oil-producing nuts and seeds, rubber, hardwoods in the form of logs or lumber, dyewoods and other tanning materials, and quinine and other drugs.

Some of the Latin American countries are largely dependent upon the export of a single agricultural product, or a very few such products. In 1938 exports from all of the Central American countries, the three West Indian republics, and all of the South American countries except Bolivia, Chile, Peru, and Venezuela consisted in large part, if not entirely, of agricultural (not including pastoral) products. The four countries named and Mexico export a larger proportion of mineral products than of agricultural products. The export trade of Colombia and Ecuador is composed of substantial proportions of both agricultural and mineral products, and that of Uruguay consists chiefly of pastoral products.

In 1938, agricultural products (not including pastoral) accounted for more than 47 percent of all Argentine exports; three products - corn, wheat, and linseed - accounted for 39 percent. Other important agricultural or forest products were oats, barley, wheat flour, bran, and quebracho extract. In 1938 exports of coffee from Brazil constituted 45 percent of that country's total exports, amounting to 296 million dollars; four agricultural and forest products - coffee, cotton, cacao, and oil-producing seeds and nuts - accounted for over 70 percent of its total export trade. Paraguay, in 1938 exported products valued at over 8 million dollars, 27 percent of which consisted of raw cotton, 18 percent of quebracho extract, and 7 percent of yerba mate', or a total of about 52 percent for these three products. From Colombia exports in 1938 were valued at 81 million dollars, of which over 61 percent consisted of coffee and 6 percent of bananas. Of Ecuador's total exports, approximating 13 million dollars in 1938, 23 percent consisted of cacao, 10 percent of coffee, 6 percent of rice, and over 4 percent of tagua, or a total of nearly 44 percent for these four products.

Agricultural and forest commodities account for even larger proportions of the exports of the Central American area. Nearly 85 percent of Costa Rica's export trade in 1938 consisted of three commodities - coffee, bananas, and cacao. In 1937 over 90 percent of El Salvador's export trade consisted of coffee. Approximately 90 percent of the export trade of Guatemala in 1938 was accounted for by two commodities - coffee and bananas; these commodities also constituted nearly 60 percent of the export trade of Honduras in that year.

The West Indian republics are similarly dependent upon the export of one or a few agricultural and forest products. In 1938 nearly 80 percent of Cuba's total export trade consisted of sugar and sugar products. The Dominican Republic is largely dependent on three commodities - raw sugar, cacao, and coffee - which in 1938 constituted 81 percent of its exports.   The export trade of Haiti is more diversified than that of Cuba or the Dominican Republic, but in 1938 agricultural products accounted for 97 percent of its total shipments to foreign countries.

Pastoral industries. - Cattle raising has been carried on in most parts of Latin America since the beginning of the colonial period. Aided by the development of refrigeration facilities, improved stock, and cheaper and more adequate transportation, stock raising and its allied industries have expanded rapidly.   Latin America now accounts for approximately two-thirds of all the fresh, chilled, and frozen beef which enters international trade, about one-fifth of the mutton and lamb, and nearly all of the canned beef.   The Latin American countries also account for about 30 percent of all the cattle hides and calfskins produced in the world, about 20 percent of the sheep and lamb skins, 10 percent of the goat skins, 15 percent of the horse skins, and about 95 percent of the wild pig and hog skins;   their share of the international trade in these items is still larger.

The countries of Latin America from which exports of pastoral products are most important are Uruguay, Argentina, Paraguay, and Brazil. Of these, Uruguay is the only country from which exports are now predominantly pastoral.   Approximately 84 percent of Uruguay's exports in 1938 were the products of pastoral industry;   wool alone constituted 44 percent,   the remaining 40 percent consisted of frozen, chilled, and canned meats, hides, skins, tallow, and other animal products.   Exports of animal products from Argentina were more than 45 percent of the total exports in 1938; these exports consisted of meats, wool, hides and skins, and allied products.   In 1938, 36 percent of total Paraguayan exports consisted of pastoral products; chief among these were cattle hides, which accounted for nearly one-third of the exports of animal products.   Although appreciable quantities of animal products are exported from Brazil, such commodities are only a small percentage of total Brazilian exports (9 percent in 1938); the principal commodities are hides and skins, and frozen, chilled, and canned meats.

Mining. - In certain Latin American countries, mineral production has long been of great significance, and exports from some of these countries consist largely, or almost entirely, of mineral products. Latin America produces about one-third of the world's tin, one-third of the silver, one-fourth of the copper, and one-seventh of the petroleum.   The lack of cheap fuel has retarded the development of Latin American mineral resources.   Although the area contains substantial deposits of coal, most are inaccessible or of poor quality. Colombia, Peru, Venezuela, and Mexico have the greatest potential power resources in Latin America, inasmuch as they possess not only coal, but also petroleum and water power.

The export trade of five Latin American countries - Bolivia, Chile, Venezuela, Peru, and Mexico - is composed chiefly of minerals.   In 1938 approximately 92 percent of the total exports from Bolivia, valued at 35 million dollars, consisted of minerals, including tin which alone accounted for 68 percent.   Other metals exported were silver, lead, wolfram, zinc, antimony, and copper.   Of the total exports of Chile, amounting to approximately 141 million dollars in 1938, over 48 percent

consisted of copper bars and 22 percent of nitrates; total exports of
mineral products amounted to 78 percent of Chilean shipments to foreign
countries. In Venezuela exports of petroleum, asphalt, and their
products accounted for approximately 90 percent of that country's total
exports of 278 million dollars in 1938.[1] Over 50 percent of Peruvian
exports valued at 76 million dollars in 1938 consisted of petroleum
and copper and its concentrates. Mexico is one of the most diversified mineral-producing areas in the world. In 1938 approximately 79
percent of that country's total exports of 185 million dollars consisted of minerals and mineral products; these, in the order of their
importance, included petroleum and petroleum products, gold,[2] silver,
lead, zinc, copper, and antimony. Base metals accounted for nearly
30 percent of Mexico's total exports in 1938, the precious metals for
nearly 39 percent, and petroleum and its allied products for over 9
percent.

In 1938 exports of petroleum, gold, and platinum amounted to
approximately 35 percent of the value of total exports from Colombia.
That country is the world's second largest producer of platinum, being
exceeded only by the Soviet Union. Approximately one-third of the
exports from Ecuador (valued at nearly 13 million dollars in 1938)
were composed of minerals; chief among these were petroleum, cyanide
precipitates, silver, and gold. Exports of minerals form but a small

---

[1] Exports of petroleum from Venezuela are recorded in terms of an
official unit value which overvalues such exports by approximately
66-2/3 percent.

[2] Gold and silver are included with commodity exports by Mexico and
several other Latin American countries but are not included with commodity imports in United States statistics.

part of exports from Brazil. Brazil, however, is a producer and exporter of manganese ore, a strategic material in the production of steel. Some iron ore is also mined in Brazil, but this is consumed principally in the domestic market.

Manufacturing. - Although the economy of Latin America is primarily dependent upon the production of agricultural, pastoral, and forest commodities, and of minerals, manufacturing industries in some countries are becoming increasingly important. Manufacturing in Latin America has been retarded by the lack of skilled labor, the small population in many of the countries, and the lack of certain commodities essential to the development of heavy industries. The chief deterrents have been the quality of the coal and iron of Latin America, their inaccessibility, and the location of the two in relation to each other. Dependence upon imported coal and oil in many countries has been chiefly responsible for a localization of manufacturing at the seacoast, inasmuch as the high cost of transportation has made it unprofitable to transport these fuels to inland points.

Manufacturing in Latin America has been confined chiefly to the production of consumption goods. These include such products as cotton cloth, shoes and other types of clothing, furniture, building materials, soap, toilet preparations, cigarettes, cigars, wine, beer, rope and twine, prepared and canned meats, canned fruits, paint, matches, paper, tin cans, glassware, and household utensils. In addition, the assembling of automobiles provides employment for a substantial number of men in several countries. The larger manufacturing establishments in many of the Latin American countries are financed by foreign capital, although an increasing number of small plants has recently been established with capital of domestic origin.

The principal manufacturing industries concerned with exports are those engaged in the simple processing of mineral, agricultural, pastoral, and forest products. These include such industries as meat packing and refrigeration, flour milling, sugar extraction and re-fining, cigar manufacturing, and the crushing of oil-bearing seeds and nuts.

The countries of Latin America in which manufacturing has been most developed are Argentina, Brazil, Chile, and Mexico. These coun-tries, or the areas in them where manufacturing is principally con-ducted, are not tropical. Argentina is the leading manufacturing country in Latin America. Its industrial activity is concentrated largely in the region of Buenos Aires. In 1937, nearly 75 percent of all Argentine industry was located in the Federal District and in the province of Buenos Aires. Manufacturing establishments in Argentina produce a wide variety of fairly advanced consumers' goods, in addition to simply processed agricultural, pastoral, and forest pro-ducts, such as chilled, frozen, and canned meats, wheat flour, oils and fats, dyestuffs, and leather. Many of these establishments are small; in 1935 only 36 factories employed more than 1,000 workmen, and most of these were engaged in the production of foodstuffs and meats, or in the assembling of automobiles. Of the 40,613 industrial establishments recorded in Argentina in 1935, 29,400, or approximately 73 percent, employed 5 men or less.

Production of consumers' goods constitutes the principal part of the Brazilian industrial economy. One of the largest industries in Brazil is the textile industry. Cotton textile manufacturing is the most important branch of the industry, but woolen and rayon textiles and piece goods of hemp, jute, and flax, are also produced. Manufacturing for export, except for the processing of certain agricultural and forest products, is unimportant.

In the production of consumers' goods, Chile has attained a substantial degree of self-sufficiency. The manufacturing industries of that country rank second to agriculture in the number of persons employed; approximately 24 percent of the laboring population works in industrial plants, which are largely concentrated in the region about Santiago. More than 90 percent of all Chilean manufacturing occurs in this district. Manufacturing industries producing for export are concerned principally with the treatment of minerals, especially copper and nitrates.

Mexico produces a substantial part of its requirements of consumers' goods. In addition, there are some heavy industries manufacturing such products as structural steel, rails, car wheels, springs, nails, and wire. The largest industries of Mexico, however, manufacture foodstuffs, beverages, and the basic types of textiles; in the production of these articles Mexico is practically self-sufficient. Manufacturing industries which sell abroad are concerned principally with the simple processing of that country's mineral and forest products.

COMMERCIAL POLICY OF LATIN AMERICAN COUNTRIES

The several Latin American countries utilize most, if not all, of the various types of trade controls now employed by many nations throughout the world; in addition to customs duties, these include exchange and quota controls, bilateral agreements, official valuations, export taxes, and export subsidies. All of these controls are not employed by each of the 20 Latin American republics, and some of the controls are enforced more rigidly and are more inclusive in certain countries than in others.

There is no uniformity in the commercial policy of the 20 Latin American countries.[1] In general customs duties have been increased since 1929 and are high. In most countries they provide a large part of governmental revenue and in some countries constitute the principal source of governmental income, being designed primarily for that purpose; in others, additional sources of governmental income have been drawn upon, and tariffs have become less important from the standpoint of revenue. In certain countries where the tariff has been designed to protect and promote domestic industries, the application of the protective principle has operated to reduce customs receipts.

During the depression the decline in the value of the export trade of the Latin American countries made it difficult for them to meet the service on their foreign loans and to obtain imports

[1] See part II of this report for a discussion of the commercial policy of each Latin American country.

essential to their economies. Inasmuch as many of these countries are principally producers of agricultural products and raw materials, their situations were aggravated by the fact that the prices of their principal export commodities declined more rapidly than those of the manufactured goods which constitute a large part of their imports. Because of these adverse circumstances, several of the Latin American countries early in the decade 1930-39 adopted exchange controls and other trade restrictions in an effort to protect their financial resources and to maintain the value of their currencies.

Except for the United States, Latin American countries find their principal markets in Europe; in fact, some of the South American countries sell the major portion of their exports in European markets. During the decade 1930-39 nearly all of the countries of Europe imposed additional trade barriers which were severely restrictive, and some embraced the policy of economic self-sufficiency. Most European countries, in their effort to control and restrict imports, adopted to a greater or lesser extent such devices as exchange and quota controls and bilateral agreements. This action served to accentuate the unfavorable position of those Latin American countries which customarily sold substantial quantities of their products in Europe and has been largely responsible for their retention and expansion of trade restrictions in an effort to maintain their export markets, to secure payment for the products sold, and to safeguard their own financial structure.

In general, more South American countries maintain exchange controls than do the other Latin American countries.[1] These countries have undoubtedly found such restrictive devices less necessary than their southern neighbors, inasmuch as a very large proportion of their export trade is destined for the United States market where free exchange is readily available. Exchange controls as administered in Latin America vary widely in the extent and rigidity with which they are exercised. In some countries the rate at which foreign exchange can be bought or sold is fixed by law or decree; in others there is a multiplicity of rates, official and unofficial, the rates varying as between commodities, or countries, or both; in still others the exchange is allocated among the supplying countries and the types of commodities imported. An attempt is frequently made to allocate exchange to a given country on the basis of its importance as an export market. Under this system it is possible to favor a particular country in the amount of exchange allocated and in the rate of exchange made applicable to the imports therefrom. In similar fashion, imports of specific commodities may be favored; adequate exchange at favorable rates is made available for essential commodities, whereas others cannot be imported because little or no exchange is provided for payment. Thus the device may be, and frequently is, used to protect or encourage domestic industries.

---

[1] Among the 10 South American countries, 9 maintain exchange controls, whereas among the other Latin American countries only 4 do so.

Most Latin American countries have entered into bilateral agreements with foreign countries.[1]   These have been compensation, clearing, or barter arrangements of various kinds designed to maintain certain exports of the negotiating Latin American countries and to obtain payment therefor, to equalize the import and export trade between the signatory countries, or to provide for the exchange of surplus products.   Such agreements have been used more extensively by South American countries than by most of the others in Latin America.   Inasmuch as many Latin American countries have customarily had export trade balances with European countries, they have usually found it necessary, in order to maintain or expand their export markets, to agree to take a larger quantity of goods at favorable rates of exchange from the negotiating country.   Thus the agreements have frequently operated to reduce the opportunity of third countries to sell their products in Latin America.

Quotas, customs duties, and official valuations are employed by a number of the Latin American countries as concomitant parts of their trade control systems.   Quotas are frequently imposed in connection with the allocation of exchange to specific commodities; they have been utilized for bargaining purposes in the negotiation of commercial agreements and to limit the imports of specific

---

[1] Argentina, Brazil, and Chile are important Latin American countries which have signed such agreements; important European countries parties thereto are Germany, Italy, and, more recently, the United Kingdom.

commodities for the protection of the country's financial structure
or its individual industries, especially cotton textiles.   By
giving the Executive authority to modify rates of duty, to re-
classify articles for duty purposes, and to alter fixed valuations,[1]
the tariff has also become an important bargaining power in the
negotiation of agreements, and is so utilized by many of the Latin
American republics.

Latin American countries, like many others in recent years,
have been burdened with a surplus of certain commodities[2] and,
like others, have resorted to export subsidies in an attempt to
alleviate distress, or to meet competition in world markets from
the subsidized commodities of other countries.   This practice has
now become a part of the commercial policy of some of the Latin
American countries.[3]   Export taxes have also been utilized for
various purposes by certain of these countries.[4]   If a particular
country has a monopoly or a partial monopoly of a certain product,
it can impose an export tax on that product to provide governmental
revenue;   the tax is also employed to discourage the export of raw

---

[1] Most Latin American countries use the c.i.f. basis for valuation and thus obtain a higher duty on products subject to ad
valorem rates than if an f.o.b. basis were used; duties are further
increased, sometimes substantially, by assessing ad valorem duties
on the basis of official valuations which exceed market values.
[2] Notably coffee in Brazil.
[3] The European war, to the extent that it raises prices, may
permit the discontinuance of this practice, at least for certain
products.
[4] The Executive in Venezuela is authorized to impose an export
tax on any export product; such a tax has been imposed on exports
of tonka beans.

materials which can be processed within the country[1] and, by at least one country,[2] to recapture for the government profits arising out of increased prices for export products made possible by currency depreciation.

---

[1] For example, the export tax on henequen from Mexico, favoring the export of binder twine.
[2] Mexico. This country has also granted subsidies on imports to reduce the price of certain basic foodstuffs.

FOREIGN TRADE OF LATIN AMERICA WITH THE WORLD

General statement.

Latin America is an important world producer of tropical foodstuffs, raw materials, and minerals, and is a substantial consumer of manufactures and semimanufactures. That area is more important, however, as a supplier of products shipped in international trade than as a market for such products. This situation may be attributed in part to the debtor position of Latin America in relation to the rest of the world. During the decade 1929-38, the 20 Latin American countries shipped to foreign markets (including Latin American countries themselves) from 9 to 10 percent of total world exports and received from 6 to 8 percent of total world imports. In the period of the depression, Latin American imports declined more in relation to world totals than did exports, although the latter declined somewhat. Latin American exports, moreover, were larger in relation to total world exports in 1937 than in 1929, while Latin American imports were not. The more rapid decline during the depression of imports into Latin America than of exports therefrom occurred despite the fact that the prices of most Latin American export products declined more sharply in that period than did the prices of imported articles. It is apparent, therefore, that during the period of the depression imports into Latin America declined more abruptly in terms of quantity than did exports from that area. Indeed, the quantities

of certain products exported from some of the Latin American
countries actually increased although the total value of the exports of such products declined.   In 1937 exports from Latin
America amounted to over 10 percent of the value of total world
exports, and imports into Latin America amounted to 7 percent of
total world imports.

Exports to the world.

     In recent years the export trade of Latin America in general
has followed the course of world trade.   In the period 1929-38
exports attained their highest level in 1929, reached their low
in 1932 and 1933, and recovered substantially thereafter.   These
fluctuations, the result of world economic conditions, may be
attributed principally to changes in commodity prices, although
variations in the physical quantity of the goods exported were
also contributing factors.   Export statistics for 1929-38 are
shown in table 2.

Table 2. - Latin America: Total exports from the 20
Latin American countries, 1929-38

Year	Value	Comparison of 1929 with subsequent years	Comparison of 1932 with subsequent years
	Millions of U.S. dollars	Percent	Percent
1929	2,912.9	100.0	
1930	1,992.6	68.4	
1931	1,489.7	51.1	-
1932	1,038.8	35.7	100.0
1933	1,145.2	39.3	110.2
1934	1,676.3	57.5	161.4
1935	1,738.9	59.7	167.4
1936	1,911.5	65.6	184.0
1937	2,420.5	83.1	233.0
1938	1,833.7	63.0	176.5

Source: Compiled by the U.S. Tariff Commission from Statistical
Year Book of the League of Nations.

In 1932 Latin American exports aggregated, in terms of value,
only slightly more than one-third of those in 1929; by 1936 they
amounted to almost two-thirds, and in 1937 to over four-fifths.
The recovery of exports from the period of extreme depression was
rapid; in 1936 the value was 84 percent greater, and in 1937,
133 percent greater, than that in 1932.   Although exports declined
in 1938 and were slightly smaller than in 1936, they were still
over 76 percent greater than in 1932.   Preliminary reports indicate
that exports in 1939 were larger than in the preceding year.

South America is the principal exporting area in the Latin
American group, accounting for about 77 percent of the total export

trade. Mexico and the West Indies each contribute about 10 percent of the total, and Central America about 3 percent. During
the decade 1929-38, little change has occurred in the relative
importance of the export trade of these regions; the relationship
in 1938 was almost identical with that in 1929 (see table 3).

The export trade of Latin America is largely concentrated in
a few countries. In fact, 7 of the 20 countries accounted for 85
percent of total Latin American exports in both 1938 and 1929;
these countries, named in the order of the value of their exports
in 1938, were: Argentina (24 percent of the value of total Latin
American exports), Brazil (16 percent), Venezuela (15 percent),
Mexico (10 percent), Cuba (8 percent), Chile (8 percent), and
Colombia (5 percent). With few exceptions, the 7 countries have
maintained approximately the same relative positions throughout the
period 1929-38. Argentina ranked first in both 1929 and 1938;
in 1929 its share of that trade was 31 percent, and in 1938, 24
percent. The decline in the relative importance of Argentine
exports in 1938 was caused in part by crop failures and by a
reduction in the purchases of Argentine products by the United
States and certain European countries. Brazil maintained its
position as the second most important exporting country in Latin
America throughout the period 1929-38, and its share of total
exports fluctuated within narrow limits, ranging from 14.5 to 17
percent. Chile ranked fourth (10 percent) as an exporter among

the Latin American countries in 1929, but dropped to sixth in 1938.
The Chilean position was especially affected by the decline in the
quantity and average unit value of its exports of nitrates.   Another
country which has experienced a marked change in its position in
Latin American export trade is Venezuela.   In 1929 it ranked
sixth and its share of the trade was 5 percent; in 1938 it rose
to third and its share to 15 percent.   The rise may be attributed
principally to the substantial increase in Venezuelan exports of
petroleum.   Cuba ranked fifth as an exporter of Latin American
products in both 1929 and 1938.   The relative importance of its
position is due in part to the preferential tariff position which
it occupies in trade with the United States.[1]

Latin American exports consist chiefly of mineral, pastoral,
agricultural, and forest products; the last two groups include a
wide variety of tropical and semitropical commodities, as well as
a large number of those produced in the temperate zone.   Nearly all
Latin American exports are in the form of raw and semimanufactured
materials.

---

[1] Products imported into the United States from Cuba are accorded
rates of duty at least 20 percent below the most-favored-nation rates.
The rate of duty applicable to sugar (96°) imported from foreign countries other than Cuba is 1.875 cents per pound; the rate on comparable
sugar from Cuba is 0.9 cent per pound but imports into the United
States are limited by an absolute quota.   Cuba's second most important
export product, tobacco, is likewise accorded preferences substantially
in excess of 20 percent; imports into the United States at the reduced rates, however, are limited by a quota.

Important among Latin American exports of mineral products are crude petroleum, nitrates, tin, copper, silver, gold, and manganese. Shipments of pastoral products consist principally of meats, hides and skins, and wool. The forest products exported include a wide variety of both soft and hard woods,[1]/ and tanning materials and dyewoods. Exports of tropical agricultural products consist of cane sugar (raw and refined), coffee, cacao, chicle, bananas, tobacco, oil-bearing seeds and nuts, henequen, molasses and Brazil nuts. Other agricultural exports consist of grains including wheat, corn, barley, and oats, and cotton and flaxseed.

Most of these Latin American products are produced principally, if not entirely, for export. In fact, many of these commodities, should they lack an export market, would find only limited use within the countries which produce them. Commodity prices and the volume of foreign demand, therefore, have a profound effect upon the economies of Latin American countries.

---

[1]/ Some of the more important varieties are pine, balsa, laurel, rauli, and mahogany.

Table 3. - Latin America: Total exports 1/ from the 20 Latin American countries,
in specified years, 1929-38

(Value in millions of U.S. dollars)2/

Country	1929		1932		1936		1937		1938 3/	
	Value	Percent of total exports	Value	Percent of total exports	Value	Percent of total exports	Value	Percent of total exports	Value	Percent of total exports
Total, 20 Latin American countries 4/	2,912.9	100.0	1,038.8	100.0	1,911.5	100.0	2,420.5	100.0	1,833.7	100.0
South America	2,214.6	76.0	794.4	76.5	1,466.3	76.7	1,898.3	78.4	1,422.1	77.6
Argentina	907.6	31.2	331.4	31.9	536.1	28.0	757.4	31.3	437.6	23.9
Bolivia 5/	51.1	1.8	10.4	1.0	37.3	1.9	46.2	1.9	35.2	1.9
Brazil 6/	461.5	15.8	178.1	17.2	321.1	16.8	350.3	14.5	296.1	16.2
Chile	282.8	9.7	34.3	3.3	112.8	5.9	192.2	7.9	138.7	7.6
Colombia 7/	123.5	4.2	66.3	6.4	89.9	4.7	104.4	4.3	91.4	5.0
Ecuador 6/	17.2	.6	8.7	.8	13.9	.7	14.0	.6	11.7	.6
Paraguay	12.8	.4	7.5	.7	7.1	.4	9.0	.4	8.0	.4
Peru	116.8	4.0	37.1	3.6	83.3	4.4	93.2	3.8	77.2	4.2
Uruguay	92.0	3.2	27.4	2.6	72.1	3.8	78.0	3.2	58.9	3.2
Venezuela 6/	149.3	5.1	93.2	9.0	192.7	10.1	253.6	10.5	267.3	14.6
Central America	101.1	3.5	48.8	4.7	50.9	2.7	62.1	2.6	58.7	3.2
Costa Rica 7/	18.2	.6	8.5	.8	8.3	.5	11.5	.5	11.8	.6
El Salvador 7/	18.4	.6	5.5	.5	10.1	.5	15.6	.6	13.5	.7
Guatemala 5/	24.9	.9	10.7	1.0	15.0	.8	16.1	.7	16.4	.9
Honduras 7/ (fiscal years)	24.6	.9	17.6	1.7	9.1	.5	9.6	.4	8.5	.5
Nicaragua 7/	10.9	.4	4.5	.5	4.2	.2	5.2	.2	4.6	.3
Panama	4.1	.1	2.0	.2	4.2	.2	4.1	.2	3.9	.2
Mexico 7/	284.6	9.8	97.3	9.4	215.4	11.3	247.5	10.2	186.1	10.1
West Indies	312.6	10.7	98.3	9.4	178.9	9.3	212.6	8.8	166.8	9.1
Cuba	272.4	9.3	79.9	7.7	154.7	8.1	185.8	7.7	144.5	7.9
Dominican Republic 8/	23.5	.8	11.2	1.0	14.7	.7	17.8	.7	15.4	.8
Haiti 8/ (fiscal years)	16.7	.6	7.2	.7	9.5	.5	9.0	.4	6.9	.4

1/ Unless otherwise stated, the figures represent special trade, merchandise only, i.e., bullion and specie are excluded.
2/ Conversion rates are based on the U.S. dollar containing 23.22 grains of fine gold in 1929 and 1932, and 13.71 grains of fine gold in 1936, 1937, and 1938.
3/ Wholly or partly estimated.
4/ Ratio of total exports from Latin American countries to total world exports (exclusive of Spain): 1929, 8.9 percent; 1932, 8.2 percent; 1936, 9.1 percent; 1937, 9.3 percent; and 1938, 8.1 percent.
5/ Includes bullion and specie.
6/ General exports.
7/ General exports, including bullion and specie.
8/ Includes bullion.

Source: Compiled by the U.S. Tariff Commission from Statistical Yearbook of the League of Nations.

Imports from the world.

As with exports, imports into Latin America attained a peak in 1929;
they declined sharply thereafter and reached a low point for the decade
1929-38 in 1932.   After 1932, Latin American import trade recovered appreciably, but did not regain the levels attained in 1929. These fluctuations, the result of world economic conditions, may be attributed both
to changes in commodity prices and to variations in the physical quantity
of the goods which moved in foreign trade.   Import statistics for specified years, 1929 to 1938, are shown in table 4.

Table 4. - Latin America: Total imports into the 20 Latin American
countries, 1929-38

Year	Value	Comparison of 1929 with sub- sequent years	Comparison of 1932 with sub- sequent years
	Millions of U.S. dollars	Percent	Percent
1929 ———————	2,425.0	100.0	
1930 ———————	1,791.5	73.9	—
1931 ———————	1,024.2	42.2	—
1932 ———————	618.7	25.5	100.0
1933 ———————	781.8	32.2	126.4
1934 ———————	1,027.9	42.4	166.1
1935 ———————	1,135.2	46.8	183.5
1936 ———————	1,241.0	51.2	200.6
1937 ———————	1,656.9	68.3	267.8
1938 ———————	1,488.5	61.4	240.6

Source: Compiled by the U. S. Tariff Commission from Statistical
Year Book of the League of Nations.

In 1932 imports into Latin America aggregated only about one-fourth of the value of those in 1929;   by 1936 they amounted to one-half of the imports in 1929, and in 1937 to more than two-thirds. Latin American imports were 100 percent greater in 1936, and 168 percent greater in 1937 than in 1932.   Although imports declined somewhat in 1938, they did not decline as rapidly as exports and were still 140 percent greater than in 1932.   Price changes account in part for the variations in imports, but are not so important as in exports.

South America customarily accounts for over 75 percent of all Latin American imports (79 percent in 1938).   Mexico and the West Indies each purchase from 7 to 10 percent of the total, and Central America about 5 percent (see table 5).   During the decade 1929-38 little change took place in the relative position of three of these areas as markets for imports, their share in 1938 being almost identical with that in 1929.   The share of the West Indian republics in imports, however, fell from 10.6 percent to 8.3 percent of the total.

The seven leading exporting countries in Latin America are also the seven largest purchasers of foreign goods;   in 1938, and in 1929 as well, they accounted for approximately 84 percent of all Latin American imports.   Although these seven countries were the principal sellers and purchasers in foreign markets, they did not hold the same relative rank in both of these phases of Latin American foreign trade. Named in the order of the value of their imports in 1938, the seven leading countries were: Argentina (30 percent of the value of total Latin American imports), Brazil (20 percent), Mexico, Cuba, Venezuela, and Chile (7 percent each), and Colombia (6 percent).   Of these countries, Venezuela showed the greatest relative increase in 1938 as compared with 1929. In 1929, it ranked seventh among the importing countries of Latin America and accounted for only 4 percent of all imports into that area; in 1938 it ranked fourth, with 7 percent of the total. Other countries which increased their participation in the import trade of Latin America were Brazil (17 percent in 1929 and 20 percent in 1938) and Colombia (5 percent in 1929 and 6 percent in 1938). The other four leading countries - Argentina, Mexico, Cuba, and Chile - declined in importance as markets for imports.

Imports into Latin America are largely complementary to production in that area. Latin American countries produce for local consumption principally basic foodstuffs and, in a few of the more industrialized countries, manufactured goods for direct consumption, such as textiles, clothing, hosiery, and shoes; some of the industrialized countries also produce, though in limited quantities, durable consumption goods and production goods. For export, these countries rely almost entirely on raw materials derived from agriculture and livestock, forests, and mines. Imports into Latin American countries are almost infinite in their variety and include both consumption and production goods. The proportion of total imports represented by either one of these two groups and the type of goods imported within each group vary from country to country and are dependent in large part upon the economy of each country and the purchasing power and habits of its people. Imports of consumption goods include both nondurable consumption goods, such as textiles, clothing, and prepared foodstuffs (for example, canned fruits, milk, and fish, and wheat flour), and durable consumption goods, such as radios, electric refrigerators, automobiles, tires, and other rubber goods.[1] Imports of production goods are also diversified. They include chemicals; petroleum; coal; agricultural and industrial machinery; motors (gasoline and electric); electrical equipment; sewing machines; office equipment and appliances; airplanes; railroad locomotives, cars, and equipment; and finished and semifinished iron and steel products.

Many of the Latin American countries are attempting to develop manufacturing industries within their own boundaries. To the extent that they are successful in this endeavor, the imports of some products will probably be curtailed. But should the standard of living and purchasing power of the Latin American people be improved by these efforts, the import trade of Latin America, though changed somewhat in character, would probably expand rather than contract.

---

[1] Imports of consumption goods are purchased by a small proportion of the population of Latin American countries, principally people in the large cities. The limited purchasing power of most people in Latin America does not permit the acquisition of imported articles.

Table 5. - Latin America: Total imports 1/ into the 20 Latin American countries, in specified years, 1929 to 1938

(Value in millions of U. S. dollars) 2/

Imported from -	1929 Value	1929 Percent of total imports	1932 Value	1932 Percent of total imports	1936 Value	1936 Percent of total imports	1937 Value	1937 Percent of total imports	1938 3/ Value	1938 3/ Percent of total imports
Total, 20 Latin American countries 4/	2,425.0	100.0	618.7	100.0	1,241.0	100.0	1,656.9	100.0	1,488.5	100.0
South America	1,870.6	77.1	455.8	73.7	928.7	74.8	1,257.3	75.9	1,182.2	79.4
Argentina	819.5	33.8	215.2	34.8	347.0	28.0	482.1	29.1	442.6	29.7
Bolivia 5/	26.1	1.1	4.7	.8	20.6	1.7	22.0	1.3	24.4	1.6
Brazil 6/	421.7	17.4	105.8	17.1	247.1	19.9	334.3	20.2	292.7	19.7
Chile	196.8	8.1	26.0	4.2	71.3	5.7	88.3	5.3	103.2	6.9
Colombia 7/	123.0	5.1	29.2	4.7	68.4	5.5	96.1 :8/	5.8 :8/	88.0	5.9
Ecuador 6/	16.8	.7	4.3	.7	11.1	.9	11.0	.7	10.3	.7
Paraguay	13.2	.5	3.8	.6	7.3	.6	9.3	.6	8.1	.5
Peru	76.0	3.1	17.6	2.9	50.2	4.0	60.1	3.6	59.4	4.0
Uruguay 9/	92.0	3.8	26.1	4.2	52.7	4.2	63.6	3.8	48.6	3.3
Venezuela 6/	85.5	3.5	23.1	3.7	53.0	4.3	90.5	5.5	104.9	7.1
Central America	114.3	4.7	39.0	6.3	64.0	5.2	79.4	4.8	72.6	4.9
Costa Rica 7/	20.2	.8	5.5	.9	8.4	.7	11.8	.7	12.2	.8
El Salvador 7/	17.8	.7	5.2	.8	8.4	.7	10.3	.6	9.1	.6
Guatemala 7/ (fiscal years)	30.4	1.3	7.5	1.2	14.4	1.2	21.0	1.3	21.0	1.4
Honduras 7/ (fiscal years)	14.9	.6	8.4	1.4	8.3	.7	10.3	.6	9.1	.6
Nicaragua 7/	11.8	.5	3.5	.6	5.1	.4	4.2	.3	3.6	.3
Panama 6/	19.2	.8	8.9	1.4	18.9	1.5	21.8	1.3	17.6	1.2
Mexico 7/	184.2	7.6	57.6	9.3	127.7	10.3	170.2	10.3	110.0	7.4
West Indies	255.9	10.6	66.3	10.7	120.6	9.7	150.0	9.0	123.7	8.3
Cuba 6/	216.2	8.9	51.0	8.2	103.2	8.3	129.4	7.8	105.9	7.1
Dominican Republic 10/	22.5	1.0	7.8	1.3	9.8	.8	11.5	.7	10.2	.7
Haiti 10/ (fiscal years)	17.2	.7	7.5	1.2	7.6	.6	9.1	.5	7.6	.5

1/ Unless otherwise stated, the figures represent special trade, merchandise only, i.e., bullion and specie are excluded.
2/ Conversion rates are based on the U.S. dollar containing 23.22 grains of fine gold in 1929 and 1932, and 13.71 grains of fine gold in 1936, 1937, and 1938.
3/ Wholly or partly estimated.   4/ Ratio of total imports into Latin American countries to total world imports (exclusive of Spain): 1929, 6.9 percent; 1932, 4.5 percent; 1936, 5.6 percent; 1937, 6.0 percent; and 1938, 6.2 percent.
5/ Includes bullion and specie.   7/ General imports, including bullion and specie.
6/ General imports and specie.   9/ Official values.   10/ Includes bullion.
8/ After 1936, includes freight.

Source: Compiled by the U. S. Tariff Commission from Statistical Year Book of the League of Nations.

Principal markets for Latin American exports and sources of
Latin American imports.

Among the principal industrial nations of the world, the United
States is by far the largest market for exports from Latin America
(see table 6), in recent years having taken approximately one-third of
all Latin American products shipped abroad.   In 1938 the United States
accounted for 30.2 percent of the export trade of that area, the United
Kingdom for 16.8 percent, Germany for 10.5 percent, France for 4.1 percent, Italy for 1.6 percent, Japan for 1.3 percent, and all other countries (including Latin American countries) for 35.5 percent.   During
the decade 1929-38, the United States and the United Kingdom maintained
their positions as leading markets for Latin American goods, though
they declined somewhat in relative importance;   Germany and Japan increased in importance, while France and Italy declined.   These six
countries took 70 percent of Latin American exports in 1929 and 65 percent in 1938.

The United States is also the principal supplier of commodities
imported into Latin America (see table 6).   In 1929 the share of the
United States in the Latin American market was 38.5 percent;   in 1932
it declined to 32.1 percent, and since that time has remained at approximately the same level (33.9 percent in 1938).   The share of the
United Kingdom in the import trade of Latin America declined from 16.3
percent in 1932 to 11.7 percent in 1938.   Germany, however, increased
its participation from 9.5 percent in 1932 to 16.2 percent in 1938.
These three countries supplied over 60 percent of total Latin American
imports in 1938.   Among the other important industrial countries,

France, Italy, and Japan, each supplied approximately 3 percent.   Of
these three countries, only Japan increased its share of the trade
during the period 1929-38.   The six leading industrial countries supplied approximately 70 percent of Latin American imports in 1938.

Table 6. - Latin America: Foreign trade of the 20 Latin American countries with selected countries, in specified years, 1929 to 1938

(Value in thousands of U.S. dollars)

Country	1929 Value	1929 Percent of total	1932 Value	1932 Percent of total	1936 Value	1936 Percent of total	1937 Value	1937 Percent of total	1938 1/ Value	1938 1/ Percent of total
Exports to:										
All countries 2/	2,912,270	100.0	1,041,252	100.0	1,826,857	100.0	2,329,153	100.0	1,802,300	100.0
UNITED STATES 4/ 5/	988,054	33.9	332,512	31.9	605,882	33.2	719,579	30.9	543,989	30.2
United Kingdom	535,904	18.4	203,448	19.5	343,405	18.8	410,588	17.6	302,457	16.8
Germany	234,775	8.1	76,914	7.4	148,974	8.1	204,336	8.8	188,915	10.5
Japan	3,818	.1	1,109	.1	35,988	2.0	37,956	1.6	24,128	1.3
Italy	91,399	3.1	32,736	3.2	32,440	1.8	70,768	3.0	28,383	1.6
France	181,794	6.3	69,768	6.7	91,831	5.0	94,935	4.1	73,487	4.1
All other countries	876,526	30.1	324,765	31.2	568,337	31.1	790,991	34.0	640,941	35.5
Imports from:										
All countries 2/	2,415,298	100.0	619,362	100.0	1,201,956	100.0	1,624,205	100.0	1,467,071	100.0
UNITED STATES 4/	931,014	38.5	198,857	32.1	385,704	32.1	552,259	34.0	498,305	33.9
United Kingdom	362,039	15.0	101,197	16.3	167,709	13.9	214,572	13.2	171,228	11.7
Germany	261,944	10.8	58,721	9.5	188,058	15.7	250,275	15.4	237,794	16.2
Japan	14,767	.6	6,442	1.0	35,860	3.0	46,362	2.8	37,679	2.6
Italy	113,411	4.7	33,711	5.5	24,155	2.0	38,257	2.4	43,918	3.0
France	124,479	5.2	30,408	4.9	39,799	3.3	48,518	3.0	48,267	3.3
All other countries	607,744	25.2	190,026	30.7	360,671	30.0	473,962	29.2	429,880	29.3

1/ Preliminary.
2/ Trade statistics of Honduras in 1929-37 are for fiscal years ended July 31; in 1938, by governmental decree, they are for the 11 months ended June 30. Data for Haiti are for fiscal years ended September 30.
3/ Exports from El Salvador to the United Kingdom, Japan, Italy, and France are included in "All other countries."
4/ Trade of Costa Rica with the United States includes Panama in 1929 and 1932.
5/ Gold shipments are excluded from Colombian exports as follows: 1929 - $5,026,397 (to the U.S., $5,013,077); 1932 - $2,941,292; 1936 - $11,884,381; 1937 - $18,109,757; and 1938 - $10,503,879, all to the United States.

Source: Compiled by the U.S. Tariff Commission from official statistics of the 20 Latin American countries.

FOREIGN TRADE OF LATIN AMERICA WITH THE UNITED STATES

General statement.

The trade between Latin America and the United States rests chiefly upon the diversity of the commodities produced in the two regions. This dissimilarity arises from differences in climates, in natural resources, and in economic development.

Latin America in large part is situated in the tropical zone and is a leading world producer of tropical foodstuffs and raw materials. Moreover, it is largely a non-industrial area. The United States, on the other hand, is situated in the temperate zone and is highly industrialized; its export products are mainly manufactures and agricultural products common to temperate agricultural regions. Trade between the two regions has consisted essentially of the exchange of Latin American tropical foodstuffs and industrial raw materials for United States manufactures and semimanufactures.

Northward to United States markets move coffee, sugar, bananas, chicle, tobacco, henequen, and many other tropical products; gold, silver, copper, petroleum, nitrates, and other minerals; and flaxseed, wool, hides, skins, and certain other agricultural and pastoral products, the production of which in this country is insufficient for home requirements. Major exports from the United States to Latin America are automobiles, trucks, mining machinery, electrical machinery, agricultural equipment, cotton cloth, and wheat flour.

Although the trade in the main is complementary, it is not entirely so, and therefore major problems affecting commerce between the

two regions have arisen.   A part of Latin America is situated in the
temperate zone, and in large measure the agricultural and pastoral output of this section is similar to that of the United States; the two
regions produce many of the same minerals; and certain countries, including Argentina, Brazil, Mexico, and Cuba, are undergoing rapid industrialization.   All of these factors operate to reduce the complementary nature of the products of Latin America and of the United
States.   Latin America, however, remains an indispensable source of
foodstuffs and raw materials not produced in the United States, and is
also an essential supplementary source of numerous raw materials available in the United States but produced in insufficient quantities to
satisfy domestic requirements.   Moreover, Latin America despite its
industrial development still requires many of the products manufactured
in the United States.

Though the trade is based in large part on permanent geographic
factors, significant alterations in the nature and distribution of
United States trade with Latin America have occurred in the last decade.   United States imports from Latin America have become more diversified.   For example, imports of coffee decreased from 85 percent of
the total value of imports from Brazil in 1932 to a low of 59 percent
in 1937.   Products now comprising an increased share of this trade include, among others, babassu nuts, cottonseed oil, canned beef, and
cattle hides.   Equally important changes have occurred in the composition of United States exports to Latin America as a result of the
accelerated rate of industrialization in Latin America, the recent

broadening of purchasing power, and the technological development of
new products.   Increased industrialization in Argentina, Brazil, Cuba,
and Mexico, in recent years accounts for increased exports to some of
these countries of machinery of various types and such semimanufactures
as steel plates and sheets, cotton yarn, caustic soda, tin plate, and
petroleum.   Improved economic conditions in many Latin American countries have resulted in increased United States exports of radio sets
and parts, household electric refrigerators, and motion-picture films.

Fluctuations in the world prices of Latin America's great income-
producing commodities have been of outstanding importance in determining the value of trade of that region with the United States and with
the rest of the world.   In the last 10 years the variations in the
value of United States imports from Latin America reflect largely
fluctuations in prices, although fluctuations in physical volume have
been of considerable importance in influencing the trade of certain
commodities such as minerals, wool, hides and skins, flaxseed, and
corn.   The supplies forthcoming each year of the principal tropical
foodstuffs, such as sugar, coffee, bananas, and cacao are fairly fixed
and not readily adjusted to changes in market conditions.   Even mod-
erate changes in the demand for these products have led to great fluctuations in prices, since the demand for them is inelastic; that is,
the volume of sales does not respond readily to changes in prices.
Hence, when the world demand for Latin American foodstuffs decreased,
as it did after 1929 when business conditions were depressed, the somewhat reduced volumes of Latin American exports of these goods brought
very greatly reduced prices.   There was, therefore, a great decline

in the value of United States imports from Latin America. And when
the world demand increased after 1932 there was a marked increase in
the value of imports. Under the circumstances, the fluctuations in
the purchasing power of the exporting countries in Latin America have,
of course, been large and have had a decided effect upon the capacity
of this area to import goods from the United States and elsewhere, to
make payments on foreign debts and investments, and to maintain stable
currencies and public finance.

Widely fluctuating world prices for the principal Latin American
exports in the last decade together with fluctuations in world consumption of some of these products, have had a crucial effect upon the
capacity of the Latin American countries to make interest payments to
United States holders of dollar bonds (having, as of 1936, a par value
of about 1.1 billion dollars, or 30 percent of total United States
holdings of foreign dollar bonds) and to transfer income to United
States owners of direct investments in Latin America (valued at about
2.8 billion dollars, or 43 percent of total United States direct investments in foreign countries).[1] Foreign exchange available for
such payments has customarily been derived in large part from Latin
America's excess of exports in its trade with the United States, but
during the last decade the trade balances of many of the Latin American
countries with the United States have fluctuated widely because of
changes in the world prices of major Latin American products and in
the demand for certain of them in the United States. At the same

[1] See Balance of International Payments of the United States in
1938, appendix D, p. 90, and American Direct Investments in Foreign
Countries - 1936, table 1, p. 5, U. S. Department of Commerce.

time, many of these countries had outstanding large amounts of dollar bonds obligating them to pay interest charges which were fixed in amount. The effects of this situation upon the Latin American countries were particularly conspicuous in the period 1930-33, when most countries defaulted on interest and sinking fund payments and many established rigid government control of foreign exchange and trade.

Trade of Latin America with the United States, by regions.

In analyzing the trade of Latin America with the United States, the countries of that area may be segretated into four geographic regions or groups. These are (1) the Caribbean countries, consisting of Colombia, Venezuela, the Central American countries, Mexico, and the West Indian republics; (2) Brazil; (3) the west coast South American countries consisting of Bolivia, Chile, Ecuador, and Peru; and (4) the east-coast temperate-zone South American countries consisting of Argentina, Paraguay, and Uruguay (see table 7). Among these groups the importance of trade with the United States in relation to total trade (import and export combined) is greatest in the Caribbean area where it averages approximately 50 percent. In Brazil trade with the United States constitutes about 30 percent of the total, in the west coast South American countries, nearly 25 percent, and in the east coast countries over 10 percent.

In the Caribbean group exports to the United States in terms of value have customarily exceeded imports therefrom; nevertheless, exports to the United States have accounted for a smaller share of total exports than have imports from the United States of total imports. In the trade of Brazil, exports to the United States have also exceeded imports, but in the trade of the west coast and the east coast South American countries, imports from the United States have generally been larger than exports thereto. The trade of some of the countries differs considerably from that of others in the same group. This is especially true of the west coast South American countries. The trade of Ecuador, for example, is quite different from that of other countries in the group. Among the Caribbean countries the trade of Venezuela and Mexico differs from the others, inasmuch as minerals constitute an important part of the exports of these two countries.

Exports to and imports from the United States of the 20 Latin American countries in 1938, arranged on a regional basis, are shown in table 7. The proportion of the trade of each country accounted for by trade with the United States is also shown.

Table 7. - Trade of the United States with the 20 Latin
American countries, 1938

(Value in thousands of U. S. dollars)

Country	Imports from the United States		Exports to the United States	
	Value	Percent of total	Value	Percent of total
Caribbean countries:				
Mexico	63,027	57.7	124,944	67.4
Cuba	75,152	79.9	108,363	76.0
Dominican Republic	6,072	5 .5	4,607	32.1
Haiti	4,126	54.3	2,972	42.8
Costa Rica	6,195	49.1	4,628	45.6
El Salvador	4,275	46.7	6,756	61.8
Guatemala	7,492	44.7	11,34	69.4
Honduras	5,871	62.0	6,362	86.5
Nicaragua	3,058	5 .7	3,961	67.3
Panama	10,139	5 .6	3,34	89.2
Colombia	45,643	5 .2	42,60	52.7
Venezuela	54,939	5 .4	36,85	13.2
Brazil	71,576	24.2	101,458	34.3
West coast South American **countries:**				
Bolivia	6,556	25.5	1,595	4.6
Chile	28,620	27.7	20,45	14.6
Ecuador	3,828	4.6	4,73	37.5
Perú	20,005	4.3	20,560	26.3
East coast, temperate zone **South American countries:**				
Argentina	75,832	17.6	35,266	8.5
Paraguay	60	9.8	2,10	12.2
Uruguay	5, 39	1	, 80	4.0

Source: Compiled by the U. S. Tariff Commission from official statistics of the 20 Latin American countries.

The Caribbean countries. - In 1938 the Caribbean countries as a group purchased from the United States 55 percent of all their imports (total imports amounted to nearly 500 million dollars), and sold to the United States over 45 percent of all their exports (amounting in that year to 750 million dollars). The prominent position occupied by the United States in the trade of these countries is due to a number of factors; among these may be mentioned the character of the commodities which these countries produce and the large demand in the United States for such products, the capital invested by United States citizens in these countries, their proximity to the United States, the direction of the principal trade.routes, the availability of shipping services, and the formal or informal relationship existing between their currencies and the United States dollar.

Except for northern Mexico, the countries bordering the Caribbean Sea are located in the tropics. Consequently, the agricultural and forest commodities which they produce are largely complementary to, rather than competitive with, those produced in the United States. Outstanding exceptions are tobacco and sugar, the largest exports from this area, in terms of value. Exports of sugar, however, supplement United States production, which has always been inadequate to United States requirements; and exports of tobacco differ from, and are complementary to, most of the types grown in the United States. Other principal agricultural and forest products exported from this region are coffee, cacao, bananas, chicle, henequen, and cabinet woods (principally mahogany). These commodities are not produced in the United States and are entered free of duty   The United States market for such products is large and the Caribbean countries furnish it with substantial quantities. Indeed, the United States is the principal export market for each of the Caribbean countries, except Venezuela.[1]

The principal mineral products exported by the Caribbean countries are petroleum, and gold and silver. Petroleum is most important in the export trade of Venezuela, but that country sells only about 15 percent of its petroleum exports directly to the United States, inasmuch as Venezuelan petroleum is refined principally in the Netherlands West Indies and is subsequently exported from there in its refined form. Moreover, the United States import excise tax, imposed on petroleum and petroleum products in 1932, has operated to curtail the sale (whether direct or indirect) of Venezuelan petroleum in the United States.[2] Most of the gold and silver mined in the Caribbean area, however, has found its way to the United States because in recent years such metals could be disposed of most advantageously in that market.

Substantial amounts of capital have been invested by citizens of the United States in the production of certain of the principal export commodities of the Caribbean countries, especially sugar, bananas, chicle, petroleum, and silver. Of the 2,847 million dollars invested in Latin America by United States citizens (as of 1936), 1,675 million dollars, or 59 percent, was invested in Caribbean countries. This

[1] Venezuela would be less conspicuous as an exception if the crude petroleum shipped from that country to the Netherlands West Indies and thence in refined form to the United States could be included in the export statistics of the country of origin.

[2] The import excise tax on crude petroleum was $\frac{1}{2}$ cent per gallon. In the trade agreement with Venezuela this tax was reduced to $\frac{1}{4}$ cent per gallon so long as the total quantity of crude oil and fuel oil entering the United States in any calendar year is not in excess of 5 percent of the total quantity of crude oil processed in refineries in continental United States during the preceding calendar year.

capital has been a factor in stimulating trade, both exports and imports, between these countries and the United States. Steamship lines have been established primarily to transport the principal Caribbean export products. Once established, they have in many instances carried the lesser export products as well, and returning, have brought United States goods to be sold in Caribbean markets. The proximity of these producing areas and markets has been a factor in making this trade profitable, inasmuch as it has not been handicapped by the expenses of a long haul or by the time lag between order and delivery necessitated by great distances. In addition, the close relationship between the currencies of most of the Caribbean countries and the United States dollar has operated to give a certain degree of stability to commercial and financial transactions between the two areas.

The imports of Caribbean countries from the United States are largely complementary to production in those countries, as are their exports to production in the United States. Producing principally basic foodstuffs for local consumption, and tropical agricultural and forest products and minerals for export, the Caribbean countries must purchase abroad most of their requirements of manufactured articles, including both consumption and production goods. Many of these products are obtained almost entirely from the United States. Indeed, in each of the Caribbean countries, the United States is by far the leading supplier of total imports, and in 6 of the 12 countries accounts for over two-thirds of their total purchases abroad.

The countries having the largest trade with the United States in the Caribbean area are Mexico, Cuba, Colombia, and Venezuela; of these, Cuba ranks highest in the proportion of total import and export business done with the United States. In 1938 Cuban exports to the United States were valued at 108 million dollars and imports from the United States, at 75 million dollars. Trade between the two countries is the beneficiary of preferential tariff treatment. Moreover, sugar and sugar products exported from Cuba (accounting for 80 percent of Cuban export trade) are accorded, in addition to a substantial tariff preference, a sizable quota in the United States market. Tobacco, the other principal Cuban export product, accounts for 15 percent of total exports and is also accorded a substantial tariff preference in the United States. The two other West Indian republics, the Dominican Republic and Haiti, ship smaller proportions of their total exports to the United States than does Cuba. The principal export of the Dominican Republic is sugar, but Dominican sugar is subject to a relatively small quota in the United States and bears the full United States duty. Coffee is the leading export product of Haiti; Haitian coffee, however, is not used extensively in United States blends and is sold chiefly in European markets.

In 1938 exports from Mexico to the United States were valued at about 125 million dollars (67 percent of total exports), and imports into Mexico from the United States, at 63 million dollars (58 percent of total imports). In that year United States trade with Mexico was greater in value than that with any other Latin American country. Exports were chiefly minerals, such as silver, gold, lead, zinc, and copper, and agricultural products, such as coffee, bananas, chicle, and henequen. Proximity, trade routes, shipping facilities, and capital investments have played an important part in stimulating United States-Mexican trade.

All of the Central American countries except Costa Rica ship more than 60 percent of their total exports to the United States and buy from 45 to 60 percent of their imports from the United States. Although the trade of each of these six countries with the United States is very much smaller than that of either Cuba or Mexico, the aggregate for the group is substantial. Their principal export products are coffee, bananas, cacao, gold, and cabinet woods, all of which enter the United States free of duty. Among these countries, Panama is most dependent on the United States market; in 1938 nearly 90 percent of all its exports went to the United States. Contrary to the experience of most Latin American countries, Panama's imports from the United States, as officially recorded, customarily exceed by substantial amounts its exports to the United States. Shipments from the United States to the Canal Zone and expenditures by tourists and by the United States Army and Navy and civilians quartered in the Canal Zone doubtless account for a substantial part of this import trade balance.

Among the Caribbean countries, the trade of Colombia and Venezuela with the United States ranks next to that of Mexico and Cuba in terms of value. In 1938 the imports of Colombia and Venezuela amounted to about 45 million dollars and 55 million dollars, respectively, and the exports to 43 million dollars and 37 million dollars, respectively. Over 50 percent of the foreign trade of Colombia is carried on with the United States and over 50 percent of Venezuela's imports come from the United States. Venezuela, however, does not send a large

proportion of its exports to the United States because such exports
consist principally of crude petroleum (90 percent) which is refined
in the Netherlands West Indies and from there is shipped chiefly to
European markets, although considerable quantities are also shipped to
the United States.   Colombian exports are largely of coffee (60 percent), petroleum (25 percent), and bananas (5 percent); the first and
last of these products go largely to the United States.   Substantial
quantities of gold are also shipped from Colombia to this country.

Brazil. - In 1938, total exports from Brazil were valued at 296
million dollars and total imports at 293 million dollars.   The trade
of Brazil with the United States is the largest of any country in
South America and one of the three largest in Latin America.[1]   Over
34 percent (101 million dollars) of all Brazilian exports were shipped
to the United States in 1938, and 24 percent (72 million dollars) of
all Brazilian imports came from the United States in that year.   The
importance of the United States in Brazilian trade is due in large
part to the great demand for coffee in the United States market.   Indeed, coffee, which is the largest Brazilian export product, finds its
principal market in the United States.   Other tropical products exported to this country are cacao, babassu nuts, and brazil nuts.
Cotton, the second largest Brazilian export crop, is sold almost entirely to countries other than the United States.   This country, however, is an important market for Brazilian manganese, and hides and
skins.

---

[1] The two other Latin American countries of special importance in
trade with the United States are Mexico and Cuba.

The capital invested in Brazil by United States citizens has doubtless been a factor in stimulating United States-Brazilian trade, but such capital is much less important than that invested in the Caribbean countries. In 1936 United States investments in Brazil aggregated approximately 200 million dollars, or about 7 percent of all such investments in Latin America. Proximity to Europe, and transportation and cultural ties with that continent, have operated to make the United States less important in the trade of Brazil than in that of the Caribbean countries. Nevertheless, the United States is the chief market for Brazilian exports and the principal supplier of Brazilian imports.

Imports into Brazil from the United States consist of a large variety of consumption and production goods. Because of the development of Brazilian industries, however, production goods form a larger proportion of total imports from the United States than they do of the imports of the Caribbean countries. Brazilian imports from the United States are composed of such products as canned foodstuffs, radios, electric refrigerators, automobiles, industrial and agricultural machinery, and finished and semifinished iron and steel products.

The west coast South American countries. - In 1938, the west coast South American countries - Bolivia, Chile, Ecuador, and Peru - purchased from the United States nearly 30 percent of all their imports, amounting to 197 million dollars, and sold to the United States about 20 percent of all their exports, which approximated 263 million dollars. Although the United States has not enjoyed as large a proportion of the total trade of these countries as of the trade of the

Caribbean countries, such trade has nevertheless been influenced, though to a lesser degree, by the same factors that have affected the United States-Caribbean trade. The principal ports of the west coast South American countries are farther from the United States than are those of the Caribbean countries, yet such ports are nearer to the United States than to European markets. The total distances, however, are greater than from the Caribbean countries, and the relative advantage is smaller. In addition, the amount of United States capital invested in these South American countries is less than that invested in the Caribbean area. As of 1936, United States investments in the four countries amounted to approximately 600 million dollars, or 21 percent of total United States investments in Latin America. Moreover, trade between these countries and the United States has not been aided by the close relationship between the respective currencies which exists in the case of the currencies of the Caribbean countries and that of the United States.

Imports into the four west coast countries from the United States were valued at 58 million dollars in 1938 and their exports to the United States at 49 million dollars. Among these countries, Chile has the largest trade with the United States in terms of value; Peru ranks second, followed by Bolivia and Ecuador. With the exception of Chile, these countries are located chiefly or entirely in the tropics and their exports to the United States consist chiefly of minerals and tropical products. Imports from the United States consist of a wide range of consumption and production goods, including textiles, canned

and prepared foodstuffs, automobiles, industrial and agricultural machinery, and finished and semifinished iron and steel products.

Nearly 28 percent (29 million dollars) of all imports into Chile
were from the United States in 1938 and 15 percent (20 million dollars)
of all exports from Chile were shipped to the United States in that
year.   Chilean exports consist chiefly (80 percent) of minerals,
principally copper and nitrates.   The low prices of nitrates and of
copper have combined to reduce the value of Chilean exports to the
United States in recent years.   The United States import excise tax
on copper of 4 cents a pound prevents the consumption in the United
States of any appreciable quantity of Chilean copper but large quantities of unrefined copper are shipped to the United States to be refined
in bond and reexported to European markets.

Peruvian exports to and imports from the United States in 1938
were each valued at about 20 million dollars.   Imports from the United
States constituted 34 percent of total imports, and exports to the
United States accounted for 26 percent of the total.   Prominent among
Peruvian exports are petroleum (35 percent) and copper (15 percent);
these go chiefly to countries other than the United States.1/   The
United States, however, is an important market for Peruvian long-staple
cotton and for Peruvian sugar and wool.

Approximately one-third of the foreign trade of Ecuador (imports
and exports) is carried on with the United States.   Products shipped

---

1/ Peruvian copper is refined in bond in the United States and reexported.

to this country include coffee, cacao, cyanide precipitate, gold and silver, and straw hats.   Bolivia, though it purchases over 25 percent of its imports from the United States, sells only about 5 percent of its exports to this country.   Bolivian exports are largely (70 percent) tin, shipped almost entirely to the United Kingdom.

East coast, temperate zone South American countries. - Temperate zone countries on the east coast of South America - Argentina, Paraguay, and Uruguay - exported in 1938 products valued at over 500 million dollars and imported products valued at nearly that amount.   Of this trade, exports to the United States accounted for nearly 40 million dollars, or 8 percent of the total, and imports from the United States for about 80 million dollars, or 16 percent of the total.   The small share of the United States in the trade of these countries may be attributed to a number of factors.   Situated in the south temperate zone, they are exporters of those foodstuffs which the United States produces in large volume.[1]   From the standpoint of location they are as close to Europe as to the United States.   Moreover, United States investments in these countries are small in comparison with European investments and in comparison with United States investments in the other Latin American regions.   As of 1936, United States capital invested in Argentina, Paraguay, and Uruguay amounted to 367 million dollars, or 13 percent of all such capital invested in Latin America. Another important factor affecting the trade of this area is the large

---

[1] In years following short corn crops in the United States, notably 1937, this region has sold large quantities of corn to this country.

recent immigration into these countries from Europe and their close
cultural ties with that continent.

Of the three countries, Argentina has by far the largest trade
with the United States; Uruguay ranks second, and Paraguay third.
Indeed, Argentina in 1938 was the largest market for United States
products in all Latin America (76 million dollars), but ranked fifth
as an exporter to the United States (35 million dollars).[1] In that
year Argentina purchased about 18 percent of all its imports from the
United States and sold the United States 9 percent of its total exports. Argentine exports consist chiefly (90 percent) of cereals and
pastoral products; the chief export products are wheat and corn, flaxseed, meat and meat products, wool, hides and skins, and quebracho.
Inasmuch as most of these products are also produced in the United
States, some of them for export, Argentine commodities customarily
find their principal markets in European countries, particularly the
United Kingdom. The United States, however, is a substantial purchaser of flaxseed, canned meats, wool, hides and skins, and quebracho
extract.

Approximately 12 percent of Uruguayan imports come from the
United States, and 4 percent of Uruguayan exports are shipped to the
United States. Animals and animal products account for about 80 percent of the exports of Uruguay. European countries are the principal
export markets for these products. The United States is important

---

[1] Because of the unusual exports of corn to the United States in
1937, total Argentine exports to this country in that year were valued
at approximately 91 million dollars.

only as a consumer of canned meats, wool, and hides and skins. The
trade of the United States with Paraguay (imports and exports) is less
than that with any other Latin American country (2 million dollars in
1938). The trade in 1938, however, accounted for 10 percent of Paraguay's imports and 12 percent of its exports.[1] The principal Paraguayan export commodities are animal and animal products, cotton,
quebracho, and lumber and logs. Of these, the United States is a
significant market only for hides and skins, wool, and quebracho.

Position of Latin America in United States trade.

In the last few years trade valued at approximately one billion
dollars annually has moved between Latin America and the United States.
Although the trade of the United States with Europe and with Asia ex-
ceeds that with Latin America, nevertheless, in the aggregate United
States trade with Latin America is substantial. About one-fifth of
the value of the United States trade with the world is represented by
commerce with Latin America.

Imports. - As a source of United States imports, Latin America
holds an important position as a principal supplier of certain essential foodstuffs, minerals, and raw materials, which comprise practically all of United States imports from Latin America. Imports from
Latin America constitute somewhat more than a fifth of total United
States imports, but for a number of major commodities the ratio is far

---

[1] Much of the trade of Paraguay is indirect, through Argentina.
The share of the United States, therefore, as the original source of
imports and the final destination of exports is considerably larger
than the Paraguayan statistics would indicate. A somewhat similar,
though less pronounced situation, prevails in the case of Uruguay.

greater.   Practically all of the imports of coffee, bananas, flaxseed, sodium nitrate, quebracho extract, and cigar leaf tobacco and a large part of the imports of cacao, cane sugar, sisal and henequen, raw wool, and copper are supplied by Latin America.

In the last decade the aggregate value of imports from Latin America has fluctuated greatly but has constituted a fairly constant proportion of total United States imports.   In 1929 general imports from Latin America amounted to about one billion dollars, or 23 percent of the total; in 1933 they were only 316 million dollars, but were still 22 percent of the total.   A 4-year period of recovery followed, and in 1937 imports aggregated 672 million dollars, again 22 percent of the total.   In 1938, when imports fell to 454 million dollars, the ratio to total imports rose to 23 percent.   Imports increased to 518 million in 1939 and were 22 percent of total imports.   (See table 8.)

The continued low level of the world prices of certain major Latin American products accounts in part for the failure of aggregate United States imports from Latin America to regain, on a value basis, the level of predepression years.   The imports of certain major commodities in recent years have in fact been appreciably larger in terms of volume than in 1929, but because of lower prices, the value of such imports has been considerably smaller.   For example, the quantity of coffee imported from Latin America in 1938 was 35 percent greater than in 1929, whereas the value of imports was 54 percent smaller.

South America is the leading source of United States imports from the Latin American area; in 1938 it supplied 57 percent of all imports

from Latin America.   The West Indian republics accounted for 25 percent of such imports,[1] Mexico for 11 percent, and Central America for
7 percent.   Between 1929 and 1938 South America and Mexico declined in
importance as suppliers of United States imports, and the West Indies
and Central America increased their participation in this market.

Exports. - United States exports to Latin America, averaging in
recent years about one-half billion dollars and representing from 16
to 18 percent of total United States exports, have customarily been
somewhat smaller in aggregate value than imports therefrom and have
represented a smaller share of total United States trade.   Exports to
Latin America, however, are of particular importance to a number of
leading manufacturing industries of the United States.   Latin American
purchases represent a large part of total United States exports of
lard, wheat flour, auto tires, cotton cloth, tin plate and taggers tin,
oil-line pipe, electric household refrigerators, radio receiving sets,
mining and oil-well machinery, typewriters, agricultural implements,
harvesting machinery, automobiles, and many other products.

In the last decade the share of total United States exports going
to Latin America has been subject to greater fluctuations than has the
share of imports therefrom.   In 1929, exports (including reexports)
to Latin America amounted to 912 million dollars, or 17 percent of the
total.   They declined thereafter, and by 1932 amounted to only 195
million dollars and represented but 12 percent of total United States
exports.   During the next 5 years some recovery occurred, and in 1937

---

[1] The importance of the West Indies as suppliers of United States
imports is explained by the large imports from Cuba, the products of
which are accorded preferential tariff treatment by the United States.

exports reached 578 million dollars, representing 17 percent of the
total, the highest ratio for several years.   In 1938 they declined to
495 million dollars, or 16 percent of the total, but in 1939 rose to
569 million dollars, or 18 percent of the total.   (See table 8.)

South America is the largest market for United States products in
the Latin American area, in 1938 taking 60 percent of all United States
exports to Latin America.   In that year, the West Indian republics
accounted for 17 percent of such exports, Mexico for nearly 13 percent,
and Central America for 10 percent.   Mexico was somewhat less important as a market for United States exports in 1938 than in 1939; South
America gained in importance and the positions of the West Indian republics and Central America remained fairly constant.

Table 8. - Position of Latin America in the foreign trade of the United States, 1929-39

(Values in thousands of U. S. dollars)

Calendar year	Imports (general)			Exports (including reexports)		
	From all countries	From Latin America	Percent from Latin America	To all countries	To Latin America	Percent to Latin America
1929	4,399,361	1,014,127	23.1	5,240,995	911,749	17.4
1930	3,060,908	677,722	22.1	3,843,181	628,174	16.4
1931	2,090,635	478,164	22.9	2,424,289	312,616	12.9
1932	1,322,774	323,190	24.4	1,611,016	195,113	12.1
1933	1,449,559	316,039	21.8	1,674,994	215,680	12.9
1934	1,655,055	370,935	22.4	2,132,800	307,274	14.4
1935	2,047,485	460,997	22.5	2,282,874	344,360	15.1
1936	2,422,592	501,610	20.7	2,455,978	395,045	16.1
1937	3,083,668	672,611	21.8	3,349,167	578,203	17.3
1938	1,960,428	453,517	23.1	3,094,440	494,821	16.0
1939 1/	2,318,258	518,162	22.4	3,177,344	569,098	17.9

1/ Preliminary.

Source: Compiled from official statistics of the U. S. Department of Commerce.

<u>Position of individual Latin American countries in United States trade.</u>

<u>Imports</u>. - Imports from Latin America in recent years have amounted to more than one-fifth of total United States imports and two countries have each been the source of about 5 percent of the total. (See table 9.)   In 1939, seven Latin American countries accounted for 19 percent of United States imports; Brazil contributed 4.6 percent of total United States imports, followed closely by Cuba with 4.5 percent, and by Argentina with 2.7 percent, Mexico with 2.4 percent, Colombia with 2.1 percent, Chile 1.8 percent, and Venezuela 1 percent.   The combined imports from the remaining 13 Latin American countries represented 3 percent of total United States imports.

Between 1929 and 1939 certain shifts occurred in the position of the major individual Latin American countries in United States import trade.   The shares of imports supplied in 1939 by all of the seven countries, except Argentina, were somewhat smaller than in 1929, the share for Chile being significantly smaller.   Argentina maintained its same relative importance in both years.   Imports from most of the other Latin American countries have increased relative to total United States imports.   In general, it may be said that the principal causes for these shifts were marked fluctuations in the world prices of a few principal Latin American export products and in the United States demand for them, and changes in United States customs duties.[1]

---

[1] A more detailed discussion of these shifts will be found in those sections of part II which describe United States trade with each of the Latin American republics.

From only six Latin American countries has the United States imported as much (in terms of value) in any year during the period 1932-
39 as in 1929.   In several recent years the value of imports from
Bolivia, Guatemala, Haiti, Paraguay, and El Salvador was larger than
in 1929, and in 1937 imports from Argentina (because of the large
shipments of corn) were somewhat larger than in 1929.   However, the
value of United States imports from most Latin American countries has
recently been much smaller than in 1929; this is also true of imports
from most countries of the world.

Table 9. - United States: General imports from the 20 Latin American countries, in specified years, 1929-39

(Value in thousands of U. S. dollars)

Country	1929 Value	1929 Percent of total	1932 Value	1932 Percent of total	1936 Value	1936 Percent of total	1937 Value	1937 Percent of total	1938 1/ Value	1938 1/ Percent of total	1939 1/ Value	1939 1/ Percent of total
Total United States imports	4,399,361	100.0	1,322,774	100.0	2,422,592	100.0	3,083,668	100.0	1,960,428	100.0	2,318,258	100.0
Total United States imports from the 20 Latin American countries	1,014,127	23.1	323,190	24.4	501,610	20.7	672,611	21.8	453,517	23.1	518,162	22.3
South America	637,623	14.5	199,617	15.1	288,726	11.9	418,165	13.6	258,690	13.2	313,151	13.5
Argentina	117,581	2.7	15,779	1.2	65,882	2.7	138,940	4.5	40,709	2.1	61,920	2.7
Bolivia 2/	379	3/	6	3/	567	3/	1,363	3/	865	3/	2,029	.1
Brazil	207,686	4.7	82,139	6.2	102,004	4.2	120,638	3.9	97,933	5.0	107,243	4.6
Chile	102,025	2.3	12,278	.9	25,804	1.1	46,668	1.5	28,268	1.4	40,726	1.8
Colombia	103,525	2.4	60,846	4.6	43,085	1.8	52,345	1.7	49,398	2.5	48,983	2.1
Ecuador	5,830	.1	2,386	.2	3,331	.1	4,012	.1	2,584	.1	3,514	.1
Paraguay	529	3/	100	3/	540	3/	1,095	3/	1,336	.1	1,803	.1
Peru	30,167	.7	3,685	.3	9,023	.4	16,525	.5	12,813	.2	13,948	.6
Uruguay	18,677	.4	2,104	.2	12,232	.5	13,809	.5	4,752	.2	9,375	.4
Venezuela	51,224	1.2	20,294	1.5	26,258	1.1	22,770	.7	20,032	1.0	23,612	1.0
Central America	41,435	.9	23,829	1.8	29,299	1.2	36,008	1.2	31,394	1.6	34,995	1.5
Costa Rica	5,203	.1	3,687	.3	3,347	.1	4,434	.1	4,102	.2	3,230	.1
El Salvador	3,830	.1	1,143	.1	5,021	.2	8,563	.3	5,672	.3	6,957	.1
Guatemala	8,470	.2	4,501	.3	8,364	.3	9,611	.3	9,529	.5	10,725	.5
Honduras	12,853	.3	9,004	.7	6,078	.3	5,674	.2	5,692	.3	7,031	.3
Nicaragua	5,748	.1	1,964	.2	1,895	.1	3,103	.1	2,478	.1	2,902	.1
Panama	5,351	.1	3,530	.3	4,594	.2	4,623	.2	3,921	.2	4,060	.2
Mexico	117,738	2.7	37,423	2.8	48,938	2.0	60,120	2.0	49,030	2.5	56,319	2.4
West Indies	217,331	4.9	62,321	4.7	134,647	5.6	158,218	5.1	114,403	5.8	113,785	4.9
Cuba	207,421	4.7	58,330	4.4	127,475	5.3	148,045	4.8	105,691	5.4	104,930	4.5
Dominican Republic	8,465	.2	3,380	.3	5,354	.2	7,377	.2	5,745	.3	5,824	.3
Haiti	1,445	3/	611	.1	1,818	.1	2,896	.1	2,967	.2	3,031	.1

1/ Preliminary.
2/ Imports originating in Bolivia are credited largely to other countries. (See table 7.)
3/ Not over 0.05 of 1 percent.

Source: Compiled from official statistics of the U. S. Department of Commerce.

Imports of gold and silver. - Latin America has long been a
source of substantial United States imports of gold and silver; such
imports were valued at 152 million dollars in 1929, 156 million in
1938, and 133 million in 1939.[1] The decline in the value of the
imports in these precious metals in 1939 was caused chiefly by the
decline in price of silver and in the quantity imported in that year.
The relative importance of imports of gold and silver in United States
trade with Latin America has varied with fluctuations in the value of
imports of merchandise, being greatest when imports of merchandise
were least; in 1929 imports of gold and silver amounted to about 15
percent of the total value of merchandise imports from Latin America,
in 1938 to 34 percent, and in 1939 to 26 percent. Most of the
precious metals imported from Latin America is newly mined and as such
represents to the exporting country a commodity shipment similar to
exports of other minerals. In only a few cases (chiefly that of
Argentina) are shipments of gold and silver made from reserves to
settle international balances or to provide for the servicing of
dollar obligations.

In 1939, eight countries supplied 95 percent of all the gold and
silver imported into the United States from Latin America.[2] Mexico
alone supplied nearly 50 percent of the total; other leading sup-

---

[1] Many of the Latin American countries record their exports of gold
and silver together with their exports of merchandise; in United
States import statistics, imports of precious metals are recorded
separately.
[2] The eight countries were: Mexico, 65.6 million dollars; Colombia, 23.2 million; Peru, 11.8 million; Chile, 11.0 million;
Argentina, 5.1 million; Venezuela, 4.4 million; Nicaragua, 3.5
million; and Honduras, 2.8 million; total 127.4 million dollars.

pliers were Colombia, Peru, and Chile. From these countries, imports
of the precious metals were large in comparison with imports of merchandise. For Mexico imports of gold and silver were substantially
in excess of merchandise imports in 1939 (65.6 compared with 56.3
million dollars);[1] for Peru imports of gold and silver amounted to
nearly 90 percent of the value of merchandise imports; for Colombia
nearly 50 percent, and for Chile over 25 percent. If imports of the
precious metals are added to imports of merchandise, Mexico was the
first rather than the fourth most important source of United States
imports among the Latin American countries in 1939, and Colombia
ranked fourth rather than fifth, exceeding Argentina. Brazil and
Cuba, which were the first and second suppliers of merchandise among
the Latin American countries in 1939, drop to second and third place
when imports of gold and silver are combined with imports of merchandise.

---

[1] Imports of gold and silver also exceeded imports of merchandise
from Nicaragua in 1939 (3.5 compared with 2.9 million dollars).

Table 10. - United States general merchandise imports and imports of gold and silver from the 20 Latin-American countries, in 1929, 1938, and 1939

(Value in thousands of U. S. dollars)

Country	1929				1938				1939 [1]			
	Merchandise	Gold and silver	Total	Percent of total imports from Latin America	Merchandise	Gold and silver	Total	Percent of total imports from Latin America	Merchandise	Gold and silver	Total	Percent of total imports from Latin America
Total United States imports from the 20 Latin-American countries	1,014,127	151,793	1,165,920	100.0	453,517	155,785	609,302	100.0	518,162	133,414	651,576	100.0
South America:	637,623	99,213	736,836	63.2	258,690	69,793	328,483	53.9	313,153	59,226	372,577	57.2
Argentina [2]	117,581	72,483	190,064	16.3	40,709	32,439	73,148	12.0	61,920	5,133	67,053	10.3
Bolivia	379	4,242	4,621	.4	865	648	1,513	.4	2,029	725	2,754	.4
Brazil	207,686	-	207,686	17.8	97,933	1,465	99,398	16.3	107,243	3	107,246	16.5
Chile	102,025	2,817	104,842	9.0	28,268	9,111	37,379	6.1	40,726	10,995	51,721	7.9
Colombia	103,525	5,294	108,819	9.3	49,398	10,559	59,957	9.8	48,983	23,246	72,229	11.1
Ecuador	5,830	1,422	7,252	.6	2,584	2,667	5,251	.9	3,514	3,096	6,610	1.0
Paraguay	529	-	529	.1	1,336	-	1,336	.2	1,803	-	1,803	.3
Peru	30,167	12,321	42,488	3.7	12,813	11,418	24,231	4.0	13,948	11,785	25,733	4.0
Uruguay	18,677	251	18,928	1.6	4,752	-	4,752	.8	9,375	-	9,375	1.4
Venezuela	51,224	383	51,607	4.4	20,032	1,486	21,518	3.5	23,612	4,441	28,053	4.3
Central America:	41,435	2,638	44,073	3.8	31,394	5,714	37,108	6.1	34,905	7,857	42,762	6.6
Costa Rica	5,203	105	5,308	.5	4,102	619	4,721	.8	3,230	557	3,787	.6
El Salvador	3,830	-	3,830	.3	5,672	460	6,132	1.0	6,957	659	7,616	1.2
Guatemala	8,470	210	8,680	.8	9,529	206	9,735	1.6	10,725	171	10,896	1.7
Honduras	12,833	1,653	14,486	1.2	5,692	2,596	8,288	1.3	7,031	2,817	9,848	1.5
Nicaragua	5,748	373	6,121	.5	2,478	1,591	4,069	.7	2,902	3,521	6,423	1.0
Panama (including the Canal Zone)	5,351	297	5,648	.5	3,921	242	4,163	.7	4,060	132	4,192	.6
Mexico	117,738	49,685	167,423	14.3	49,030	79,543	128,573	21.1	56,319	65,589	121,908	18.7
West Indies:	217,331	257	217,588	18.7	114,403	735	115,138	18.9	113,785	544	114,329	17.5
Cuba	207,421	133	207,554	17.8	105,691	222	105,913	17.4	104,930	215	105,145	16.1
Dominican Republic	8,465	79	8,544	.8	5,745	507	6,252	1.0	5,824	266	6,090	.9
Haiti	1,445	45	1,490	.1	2,967	6	2,973	.5	3,031	63	3,094	.5

[1] Preliminary

[2] Argentina produces little gold and silver; imports from that country constitute chiefly shipments of monetary reserves.

Source: Compiled from official statistics of the U. S. Department of Commerce.

Exports. - The 7 countries which have been listed as the principal Latin American sources of United States imports are also the leading Latin American markets for United States exports, though not in the same order (in table 11). In 1939 Mexico and Cuba, taking approximately 2.6 percent of total United States exports, ranked first in Latin America as markets for United States products, but ranked fourth and second respectively as sources of imports. Brazil, taking 2.5 percent of total United States exports, was the third largest Latin American market but ranked first as a source of United States imports. Other important markets for United States merchandise are Argentina, Venezuela, Colombia, and Chile. Sales to these 7 countries accounted for 14.3 percent of all United States exports in 1939, while the combined value of the United States exports to the remaining 13 Latin American countries amounted to 3.6 percent of the total.

Between 1929 and 1939 some shifts occurred in the relative positions of Latin American countries in the export trade of the United States. In 1939 exports to Argentina and Chile constituted significantly smaller proportions of all United States exports than in 1929, whereas exports to Venezuela and Colombia were substantially larger in relation to the total. Changes in the scope and operation of trade and exchange controls, currency depreciation, bilateral agreements of Latin American countries with third countries, and substantial fluctuations in the national income of certain Latin American countries are among the factors contributing to these shifts.[1]

_____

[1] More specific causes of these shifts will be discussed in sections of part II describing the United States trade with individual countries.

Table 11. - United States: Total exports to the 20 Latin-American countries, in specified years, 1929 to 1939

(Value in thousands of U. S. dollars)

Country	1929 Value	1929 Percent of total	1932 Value	1932 Percent of total	1936 Value	1936 Percent of total	1937 Value	1937 Percent of total	1938 1/ Value	1938 1/ Percent of total	1939 1/ Value	1939 1/ Percent of total
Total United States exports	5,240,995	100.0	1,611,016	100.0	2,455,978	100.0	3,349,167	100.0	3,094,440	100.0	3,177,344	100.0
Total United States exports to the 20 Latin American countries	911,749	17.4	195,113	12.1	395,045	16.1	578,203	17.3	494,821	16.0	569,098	17.9
South America:	537,134	10.3	95,577	5.9	202,660	8.3	316,318	9.4	297,795	9.6	327,101	10.3
Argentina	210,288	4.0	31,133	1.9	56,910	2.3	94,183	2.8	86,793	2.8	71,114	2.2
Bolivia	5,985	.1	2,163	.1	3,564	.1	5,863	.2	5,793	.2	4,512	.1
Brazil	108,787	2.1	28,600	1.8	49,019	2.0	68,631	2.1	61,957	2.0	80,441	2.5
Chile	55,776	1.1	3,568	.2	15,739	.6	23,997	.7	24,603	.8	26,789	.8
Colombia	48,983	.9	10,670	.7	27,729	1.1	39,200	1.2	40,862	1.3	51,295	1.6
Ecuador	6,069	.1	1,754	.1	3,326	.1	5,052	.2	3,311	.1	5,900	.2
Paraguay	1,500	2/	281	2/	324	2/	743	2/	644	2/	675	2/
Peru	26,176	.5	3,962	.3	13,439	.6	19,001	.6	16,892	.6	19,246	.6
Uruguay	28,245	.5	3,217	.2	8,531	.4	13,203	.4	5,060	.2	5,177	.2
Venezuela	45,325	.9	10,229	.6	24,079	1.0	46,445	1.4	52,278	1.7	61,952	2.0
Central America:	88,863	1.7	29,619	1.8	40,403	1.7	49,619	1.5	49,341	1.6	65,256	2.1
Costa Rica	8,313	.2	2,435	.2	3,027	.1	4,477	.1	5,448	.2	9,786	.3
El Salvador	8,050	.2	2,289	.1	2,794	.1	3,628	.1	3,526	.1	4,172	.1
Guatemala	11,525	.2	2,820	.2	4,553	.2	7,612	.2	6,861	.2	8,574	.3
Honduras	12,811	.3	4,473	.3	4,900	.2	5,568	.2	6,292	.2	5,812	.2
Nicaragua	7,031	.1	1,993	.1	2,412	.1	3,353	.1	2,807	.1	4,297	.1
Panama	41,133	.8	15,609	1.0	22,717	1.0	24,981	.9	24,407	.8	32,615	1.0
Mexico	133,863	2.6	32,527	2.0	76,041	3.1	109,450	3.3	62,016	2.0	83,177	2.6
West Indies:	151,889	2.9	37,390	2.3	75,941	3.1	102,816	3.1	85,669	2.8	93,564	2.9
Cuba	128,909	2.5	28,755	1.8	67,421	2.7	92,263	2.8	76,331	2.5	81,644	2.6
Dominican Republic	14,190	.2	4,630	.3	4,578	.2	6,469	.2	5,696	.2	6,780	.2
Haiti	8,790	.2	4,005	.3	3,942	.2	4,084	.1	3,642	.1	5,140	.2

1/ Preliminary
2/ Not over 0.05 of 1 percent.

Source: Compiled from official statistics of the U. S. Department of Commerce.

Composition of United States trade with Latin America.

Trade by economic classes. - There is a marked contrast between the types of products the United States purchases from Latin America and the types it sells to Latin America. Nearly nine-tenths of the imports are composed of crude materials and foodstuffs, whereas an equally large share of exports is composed of manufactured products (see table 12). Crude foodstuffs (principally coffee, cacao, and bananas) are the leading class of imports but represent only a fraction of exports. Conversely, finished manufactures constitute only a small part of imports but account for about three-fourths of exports.

Latin America is an extraordinarily large source of imports of foodstuffs; in 1938 it supplied the United States with nearly three-fourths of all its imports of crude foodstuffs and one-third of its imports of manufactured foodstuffs (chiefly sugar). As a market for exports, however, Latin America is important particularly as a purchaser of finished manufactures (principally automobiles and machinery) and manufactured foodstuffs (including flour, lard, and canned foods); in 1938 it took more than one-fifth of total United States exports of these products.

About two fifths of the United States imports from Latin America are subject to customs duties or import excise taxes.[1] Practically all of the imports of manufactured foodstuffs, however, are dutiable, being largely of sugar. In contrast, imports of crude foodstuffs

---

[1] For a more extended discussion see section on "Tariff status of United States imports from Latin America."

are only in small part dutiable.   Imports of crude materials are
about evenly divided between the dutiable and free;   the principal
dutiable items are flaxseed, petroleum, and hides and skins, while the
leading duty-free items are sodium nitrate, carpet wool, and sisal and
henequen.   Inasmuch as copper is imported chiefly for refining in
bond and reexport, imports of semimanufactures are largely duty-free.

Table 12. - United States imports 1/ from and exports 2/ to the 20 Latin-American countries, by economic classes, 1938

	Unit	Crude materials	Crude foodstuffs	Manufactured foodstuffs and beverages	Semi-manu-factures	Finished manu-factures	Total all classes
Value of trade							
Imports	Thousand dollars:	105,014	187,864	102,892	43,124	8,510	447,404
Exports	do.	12,618	10,779	38,849	64,179	363,240	489,665
Percentage distribution							
Imports	Percent:	23.5	42.0	23.0	9.6	1.9	100.0
Exports	do.	2.6	2.2	7.9	13.1	74.2	100.0
Ratio of trade with Latin America to total United States trade							
Imports	Percent:	18.2	72.2	33.1	11.2	2.0	22.9
Exports	do.	2.1	4.3	21.1	12.7	23.9	16.0
Tariff status of imports							
Free	Percent:	47.8	93.5	1.3	84.6	74.3	60.3
Dutiable	do.	52.2	6.5	98.7	15.4	25.7	39.7

1/ Imports for consumption.
2/ Exports of domestic merchandise.

Source: Compiled from official statistics of the U. S. Department of Commerce.

Imports by commodity groups. - Imports from Latin America are
chiefly vegetable foodstuffs and, to a lesser extent, inedible vegetable
products and minerals.   Table 13 shows, for specified years 1929 to
1938, the imports into the United States from Latin America, classified
according to the 11 commodity groups adopted by the United States
Department of Commerce; also shown are percentage changes in the trade,
by commodity groups, since 1929.

Vegetable food products (chiefly sugar, coffee, bananas, and cacao)
are by far the largest of the 11 commodity groups, representing more
than 60 percent of the total value of all imports from Latin America
in 1938.   Following in importance are inedible vegetable products
(principally flaxseed, tobacco, carnauba wax, and castor beans) representing 10 percent of the total in 1938, and metals and manufactures
(chiefly copper) representing 9 percent.[1]

Between 1929 and 1932 the total value of imports from Latin
America declined 69 percent, and although there was some recovery after
1933, the value in both 1937 and 1938 remained substantially below that
in 1929.   Imports in each group, except in the small group "machinery
and vehicles," declined between 1929 and 1932.   For 7 of the 11 groups
the percentage decline was greater than for the total trade.   Among
the major groups, imports of metals showed the greatest decline,
87 percent, the result chiefly of the greatly decreased price of copper
and the reduction in demand during the industrial depression.   After

---

[1]   Gold and silver are not included in United States statistics of
merchandise trade but are included in the export statistics of some of
the Latin American countries.   If imports of gold and silver were
included in United States imports of merchandise, the proportion of the
metals group would be much higher than that shown in table 13.

1933 imports increased somewhat in value and in only two groups, namely, nonmetallic minerals (chiefly petroleum) and miscellaneous products, were they smaller in 1938 than in 1932.[1]

Imports in 5 of the 11 commodity groups in 1938 were smaller than in 1929 by a larger percentage than were total imports from Latin America.[2] The most important of these, in terms of value, is metals, imports of which were 70 percent less than in 1929; imports of nonmetallic minerals were 72 percent smaller and textile fibers (chiefly wool, sisal, and henequen), 63 percent smaller. Imports in all of the commodity groups, except nonmetallic minerals (principally petroleum) and the miscellaneous group, however, were larger in 1938 than in 1932. The greatest increases occurred in edible animal products (largely canned beef) and in chemicals and related products (chiefly nitrates). The trend of imports in large part has been determined in individual instances by special factors; for example, the curtailment of imports of nonmetallic minerals (chiefly petroleum) and of metals (chiefly copper) was in part the result of the United States revenue taxes imposed in 1932 on imports of petroleum and of copper consumed in the United States.[3] The curtailment of imports of chemicals (chiefly natural nitrate) has occurred because of the steadily increasing supplies of synthetic nitrogen available in the United States since the

---

[1] Imports from Latin America in the miscellaneous products group are principally United States products returned to this country.
[2] The decline in some of these groups was less marked in 1937 than in 1938; this is especially true of animals and animal products, inedible, vegetable products (edible and inedible), textile fibers, and metals. The decline in the imports included in these groups between 1937 and 1938 is attributable chiefly to the decline of business activity in the United States in 1938; the decline in the imports of vegetable food products, however, was caused principally by the sharp decrease in the imports of corn in 1938 following the recovery in domestic production after the drought.
[3] For a more detailed discussion of this subject, see the sections on petroleum and copper in part III.

World War.   Drastic decreases in the prices of basic commodities since 1929, with only partial recovery by 1938, have also contributed to the more than average declines in the values of imports in certain groups since 1929.

Table 13. - United States imports [1] from Latin America by commodity groups, in 1929, 1932, 1937, and 1938

Value in thousands of U. S. dollars

Commodity group	1929	1932	%	1937	1938	%	%
Animals and animal products, edible (chiefly canned beef, and cattle)	27,958	4,770	-82.9	16,482	14,754	-47.2	+209.3
Animals and animal products, inedible (chiefly hides and skins)	61,162	10,670	-82.6	34,606	14,175	-76.8	+32.8
Vegetable food products and beverages (chiefly coffee, sugar, bananas, cocoa, molasses)	535,388	218,177	-59.2	388,649	276,000	-48.4	+26.5
Vegetable products, inedible, except fibers and wood (chiefly flaxseed, tobacco, carnauba wax, castor beans, quebracho extract)	87,201	18,923	-78.3	69,545	45,369	-48.0	+139.8
Textile fibers, and manufactures (chiefly wool, sisal, and henequen)	47,608	9,349	-80.4	40,743	17,415	-63.4	+86.3
Wood and paper (chiefly cabinet woods)	2,834	736	-74.0	1,998	1,588	-44.0	+115.8
Nonmetallic minerals (chiefly petroleum)	73,883	32,807	-55.6	24,312	20,397	-72.4	-37.8
Metals and manufactures, except machinery and vehicles (chiefly unrefined copper, and manganese ore)	127,359	16,850	-86.8	57,099	37,895	-70.2	+124.9
Machinery and vehicles	96	107	+11.5	199	108	+12.5	+.9
Chemicals and related products (chiefly sodium nitrate)	40,595	4,994	-87.7	17,950	14,596	-64.0	+192.3
Miscellaneous	10,0~~			661	~~		-12.2
Total, all groups							

General imports in 1929 and 1932; imports for consumption in 1937 and 1938.

Source: Compiled from official statistics of the U. S. Department of Commerce.

Inasmuch as the United States imports from each of the Latin American countries consist largely of a few staple agricultural and mineral products, fluctuations in the quantity and value of such imports from most of the Latin American countries have appreciably affected the economies of those countries and the relative importance of certain commodity groups of imports. For example, the decline after 1929 in the value of United States imports from Latin America in the two commodity groups, animals and animal products, edible and inedible, was of great moment to Argentina, Mexico, Uruguay, and Brazil, the leading suppliers of such products. The contraction of trade values in vegetable food products, the largest group, affected principally Brazil, Cuba, Colombia, Mexico, and the six Central American countries; and the decline in the imports of inedible vegetable products affected adversely the economies of Argentina, Brazil, Mexico, and Uruguay. Argentina (wool) and Mexico (henequen), the source of four-fifths of the imports of textile fibers from Latin America, were also affected by the decline in the imports of these products, especially of wool. A number of countries were affected by changes in the value of imports of the wood and paper group (principally cabinet woods). The decline in the value of imports of nonmetallic minerals (chiefly petroleum) was of special importance to Venezuela and Mexico. Chile, Peru, Mexico, and Cuba were the principal countries affected by the decrease in the value of imports of metals, while Chile was practically the only country affected by the sharp decline in imports of chemicals (chiefly nitrates).

The proportions which imports from Latin America bear to total
United States imports by commodity groups are shown, for specified years
1929 to 1938, in table 14.   Imports from Latin America in the principal
commodity group, "vegetable food products," in 1938 were more than half
the total United States imports in this group, indicating the great
importance to the United States of Latin America as a source of foodstuffs.   The ratio of imports in only one other group, metals, was
higher than the ratio of all imports from Latin America to total United
States imports.

Although total imports from Latin America in 1938 constituted about
the same proportion of total United States imports as in 1929, imports
from Latin America in several of the groups have shifted their relative
position since 1929.   As compared with 1929, Latin America in 1938 was
a much smaller source of imports of chemicals and related products
(imports of this group from Latin America chiefly nitrates), of metals
(chiefly copper), and of nonmetallic minerals (chiefly petroleum).   As
previously noted, the revenue taxes imposed on imports of petroleum and
copper in 1932, and the development of the domestic synthetic nitrogen
industry have been contributory factors in these declines.   In only
three commodity groups has Latin America increased its share of total
imports, namely, the textile (principally textile fibers), the machinery,
and the miscellaneous groups, but these three are small compared with
total United States imports from Latin America.

Table 14. - United States imports for consumption[1]/ from
Latin America by commodity groups: Ratio of such
imports to total imports from all countries, in
specified years, 1929 to 1938

(Percent)

Commodity group	1929	1932	1937	1938 [2]/
Animals and animal products, edible	19.4	10.6	14.4	18.0
Animals and animal products, inedible	15.6	13.3	15.6	12.3
Vegetable food products and beverages	65.4	60.3	52.6	56.5
Vegetable products, inedible, except fibers and wood	15.7	15.1	14.3	15.5
Textile fibers, and manufactures	4.7	3.8	8.5	6.2
Wood and paper	.8	.4	.7	.7
Nonmetallic minerals	24.1	34.1	15.9	18.6
Metals and manufactures, except machinery and vehicles	32.2	22.7	20.3	23.9
Machinery and vehicles	.2	1.3	.8	.6
Chemicals and related products	28.2	10.4	17.5	18.7
Miscellaneous	4.6	8.1	4.6	5.6
Total, all groups	23.1	24.4	21.8	22.9

[1]/ General imports in 1929 and 1932.
[2]/ Preliminary.

Source: Compiled from official statistics of the U. S. Department
of Commerce.

Exports by commodity groups. - In sharp contrast with United States
imports from Latin America, which are chiefly foodstuffs and minerals,
all but about 5 percent of United States exports to Latin America are
manufactured and semimanufactured products. In the last few years
over half of the total exports have been represented by the combined
exports in two groups, machinery and vehicles, and metals and their
manufactures. Table 15 shows, for specified years 1929 to 1938, United
States exports of domestic merchandise to Latin America by commodity

groups. Also shown are percentage changes in the trade, by commodity groups, since 1929.

Between 1929 and 1932 the value of all exports to Latin America declined 79 percent. In general, the sharp decline in exports was spread rather evenly among the various groups. Exports of chemicals and related products decreased the least (63 percent), while exports of machinery and vehicles, by far the most important group, declined the most (87 percent).

Although exports in all groups recovered substantially after 1932, in no year thereafter did the values approach those in 1929; total exports in 1937 were 37 percent, and in 1938, 46 percent less than in 1929. Exports in some commodity groups were almost as low in 1938 as in 1932; this was true of the two groups, edible and inedible animals and animal products, which in 1938 were 70 percent less than in 1929. In certain groups, however, the recovery after 1932 was marked. Exports of chemicals and related products more than doubled between 1932 and 1938, but were 22 percent less (in terms of value) in 1938 than in 1929, and exports of machinery and vehicles increased almost fivefold between 1932 and 1938; they were, however, one-third less in 1938 than in 1929.

The divergent trends shown in United States exports by commodity groups may be attributed to a multitude of factors which have affected the effective demand for United States products in each of the 20 Latin American markets. Currency depreciation, customs duties, exchange controls, bilateral agreements with third countries, loss of purchasing power through decreased exports, and increasing industrialization have

played important roles, as have price declines in the United States.
Expanding industrialism in Latin America is partially reflected in
United States exports by the greater-than-average recovery of exports
in the metals and manufactures group after 1932.   Exports in all commodity groups, however, increased in 1938 as compared with 1932.   The
greatest increases (both relative and absolute) occurred in machinery
and vehicles, and metals and manufactures, which also experienced the
greatest decline between 1929 and 1932.   The rise in the exports of
these types of products is attributable not only to an increase in
Latin American purchasing power, but also the industrial development
in many of the Latin American countries.

Table 15. — United States exports of domestic merchandise to Latin America, by commodity groups, in specified years, 1929 to 1938

(Value in thousands of U. S. dollars)

Commodity group	1929	1932	Percentage change from 1929	1937	1938	Percentage change between 1929 and 1938	Percentage change between 1932 and 1938
Animals and animal products, edible	52,229	10,481	-79.9	13,453	14,698	-71.9	+40.2
Animals and animal products, inedible	20,259	3,909	-80.7	7,143	5,972	-70.5	+52.8
Vegetable food products and beverages	70,693	24,951	-64.7	34,971	34,726	-50.9	+39.2
Vegetable products, inedible, except fibers and wood	36,316	9,064	-75.0	20,093	16,473	-54.6	+81.7
Textile fibers and manufactures	84,892	27,986	-67.0	39,460	33,822	-60.2	+20.9
Wood and paper	47,677	9,587	-79.9	27,441	20,503	-57.0	+113.9
Nonmetallic minerals	101,564	23,613	-76.3	50,134	46,246	-54.5	+95.8
Metals and manufactures, except machinery and vehicles	99,618	17,462	-82.5	86,253	64,495	-35.3	+269.3
Machinery and vehicles	314,541	41,945	-86.7	236,293	201,152	-36.0	+379.6
Chemicals and related products	37,007	13,637	-63.2	30,547	28,772	-22.3	+111.0
Miscellaneous	37,675	10,208	-72.9	24,586	22,806	-39.5	+123.4
Total, all groups	902,471	192,843	-78.6	570,374	489,665	-45.7	+153.9

Source: Compiled from official statistics of the U. S. Department of Commerce.

The Latin American market as a whole takes approximately 16 percent of total United States exports, but purchases a substantially larger share of exports of machinery and vehicles, chemicals and related products, and edible animal products (see table 16). For a few of the commodity groups the share of total exports going to Latin America in 1938 was significantly smaller than in 1929. The ratio of exports to Latin America of inedible animals and animal products, vegetable food products, inedible vegetable products, and nonmetallic minerals declined substantially more than that of total exports to Latin America. Exports in only one group, textile fibers and manufactures, were larger in relation to total United States exports of these products in 1938 than in 1929; but the relative increase in the exports of this group to Latin America may reflect merely the more than proportionate decline in United States exports (chiefly cotton) to other world markets.

Table 16. - United States exports of domestic merchandise to
Latin America by commodity groups: Ratio of such exports
to total United States exports to all countries, in
specified years, 1929 to 1938

(Percent)

Commodity group	1929	1932	1937	1938
Animals and animal products, edible	21.4	15.1	21.6	21.2
Animals and animal products, inedible	17.2	10.3	13.3	14.0
Vegetable food products and beverages	13.9	14.5	15.9	9.6
Vegetable products, inedible, except fibers and wood	12.0	7.9	9.2	7.3
Textile fibers and manufactures	8.7	6.9	8.4	10.5
Wood and paper	22.6	16.7	20.0	21.3
Nonmetallic minerals	13.7	8.5	10.0	9.4
Metals and manufactures, except machinery and vehicles	18.6	20.6	17.2	17.8
Machinery and vehicles	26.2	18.9	26.6	23.7
Chemicals and related products	24.3	19.4	21.9	22.3
Miscellaneous	23.0	16.3	22.3	21.4
Total, all groups	17.5	12.2	17.3	16.0

Source: Compiled from official statistics of the U. S. Department
of Commerce.

Tariff status of United States imports from Latin America.

Dutiable and duty-free imports from Latin America and from all
countries. - Although several of the major United States imports from
Latin America are free of duty, being scarcely produced in this country
at all, nearly 40 percent of the total value of imports from Latin
America consists of products subject to customs tariffs or import
excise taxes. During the 3 years 1936-38, a somewhat larger proportion of the import trade with Latin America has been dutiable than of
that with the rest of the world (see table 17).

In contrast to the dutiable imports from Europe, those from Latin America are concentrated among a few products, by far the principal item being sugar, followed by flaxseed, petroleum, tobacco, hides and skins, and canned beef. Copper, though a sizable import, is only a small dutiable item, inasmuch as most of the imports from Latin America are subject to special provisions of the Revenue Act of 1932; the act provides that imports entered for smelting, refining, and export, or which come from Cuba, are duty-free. Dutiable imports of petroleum, on the other hand, are substantial; although they are also subject to the provisions of the Revenue Act of 1932, large quantities are imported for domestic consumption and not for refinement and export.

The principal duty-free imports from Latin America are coffee, bananas, cacao, sodium nitrate, cabinet woods, sisal and henequen, carpet wool, and copper (for refining and reexport).

Table 17. – United States imports for consumption[1] of free and
dutiable merchandise from Latin America and from all countries in specified years, 1929 to 1938

(Value in millions of U. S. dollars)

Year	Imports from Latin America				Total United States imports			
	Free	Duti-able [2]	Percent free	Percent dutiable	Free	Duti-able [2]	Percent free	Percent dutiable
1929 —:	679	335	66.9	33.1	2,843	1,556	64.6	35.4
1932 —:	230	93	71.3	28.7	879	444	66.5	33.5
1936 —:	267	233	53.4	46.6	1,385	1,039	57.1	42.9
1937 —:	339	318	51.6	48.4	1,765	1,245	58.6	41.4
1938 [3] :	270	177	60.3	39.7	1,183	767	60.7	39.3

[1]/ General imports in 1929 and 1932.
[2]/ Including products subject to import excise taxes.
[3]/ Preliminary.

Source: Compiled from official statistics of the U. S. Department of
Commerce.

Year to year changes in the ratios of free or dutiable trade are
the result of many factors. Fluctuations in the relative importance
of duty-free imports could be caused by the transfer of important commodities between the dutiable and the free lists, the increase of duties
to such heights as materially to restrict the importation of those
products subject to such duties, variations in industrial activity which
would increase or reduce demand for either dutiable or duty-free products,
fluctuations in the prices of dutiable and duty-free products, a temporary shortage in the United States which would impel increased importation of dutiable or duty-free products, and technological developments
or war conditions which might stimulate the demand for either dutiable
or duty-free products. All of these factors could operate to increase

the imports of dutiable products or of duty-free products; moreover, one or more of the factors might be operating in one direction at the same time that other factors were operating in the opposite direction.

In recent years the share of imports from Latin America entering the United States subject to duties has been significantly larger than in 1929 or 1932. This increase occurred in part because important commodities were made dutiable during the period 1929-38; the transfer of raw cattle hides from the free to the dutiable list in 1930, and the imposition in 1932 of import excise taxes on petroleum and its products are the leading cases of this kind.[1] The increased share of dutiable imports also reflects improved economic conditions in the United States and to a lesser extent the expansion in the trade in dutiable products resulting from tariff concessions in trade agreements concluded since 1933. Droughts in the United States in certain years have led to an increase in imports of dutiable agricultural products; most notable was the manifold but temporary increase in imports of corn from Argentina in 1937 because of the very small corn crop in the United States in 1936.

Equivalent ad valorem rates of duty. - Dutiable imports from Latin America are subject to appreciably higher average rates of duty than are such imports from the rest of the world (see table 18). The average rate of duty on sugar, which, although it is dominated by the preferential rate on imports from Cuba, is substantially higher than that on most other dutiable imports, heavily weights the average for

[1] Copper also became subject to an excise tax in 1932, but dutiable imports have been small, since most of the imported copper is for smelting, refining, and export free of duty.

all imports, since sugar represents almost one-half the value of total
dutiable imports.   Inasmuch as sugar imported from Peru, Guatemala,
Nicaragua, the Dominican Republic, and Haiti is assessed at the full
rate of duty[1]/, the average rate of duty on all dutiable imports from
these countries is far higher than on such imports from other countries
in Latin America.

Table 18. - United States imports of dutiable merchandise:
Value of imports, calculated duties, and ad valorem
rates of duty, in 1938

(Value in millions of U. S. dollars)

Dutiable imports from -	Value	Calculated duty	Equivalent ad valorem
			Percent
Latin American countries, total —	177	84	47.5
Sugar	80	43	53.8
All other dutiable imports	98	40	40.8
All other countries, total	589	217	36.8

Source: Compiled from official statistics of the U. S. Department of
Commerce, and the Bureau of Customs, Treasury Department.

Tariff status by commodity groups. - A large, and in some cases
a dominant, part of the imports from Latin America in all except 3 of
the 11 commodity groups was dutiable in 1938 (see table 19).   Imports
of metals, the largest group of commodities which were mainly free of
duty, consist chiefly of unrefined copper, coming from Chile, Peru, and
Mexico, and entered free of duty for refining and reexport; only a
small amount of dutiable copper is imported from any country, and on
most of this a drawback of duty is later paid when products made from

[1]/ The rate of duty on sugar (96°) imported from countries other than
Cuba is 1.875 cents a pound; the rate of duty on such sugar from Cuba
is 0.9 cent a pound.

it are exported. Imports in the chemicals group are largely duty-free, consisting as they do principally of sodium nitrate which is on the free list. "Miscellaneous" imports are a heterogeneous group, but, in the case of imports from Latin America, are dominated by United States products returned to this country.

The group having the highest ratio of dutiable imports in 1938 is "edible animals and animal products," consisting in large part of canned beef, coming from Argentina, Uruguay, and Brazil, and cattle coming from Mexico; both commodities are dutiable. Imports of crude petroleum, most of which is for consumption and hence dutiable, account for the large share of dutiable imports in the nonmetallic minerals group. About one-third of the imports of "vegetable food products," the largest import group, are dutiable; the chief dutiable item is sugar, imports of which are far greater in value than any other dutiable product imported from Latin America. The duty-free imports in this group consist chiefly of coffee, cacao, and bananas.

For a few commodity groups there were large changes between 1929 and 1938 in the proportion of imports subject to duty. Such shifts should be interpreted with caution. The substantially larger pro-portion of imports of "inedible animals and animal products" that was dutiable in 1938 than in 1929 was the result in part of the transfer of certain hides and skins from the free to the dutiable list in the Tariff Act of 1930. The dutiable share of imports of textile fibers has fluctuated widely since 1929 and reflects principally the great variation in imports of dutiable wool. Imposition of the import excise tax on petroleum in 1932 explains the large increase in the

dutiable imports of nonmetallic minerals. The marked decline that
occurred between 1937 and 1938 in the ratio of dutiable imports in
certain other groups resulted in part from the sharp decrease in
imports of dutiable agricultural products, the domestic supplies of
which were augmented by improved weather conditions following the
drought.

Table 19. - United States imports for consumption[1]/ of free and dutiable merchandise from Latin America, by commodity groups, in 1929 and 1938

(Value in thousands of U. S. dollars)

Commodity group	1929				1938 [2]/			
	Free	Dutiable [3]/	Total	Ratio of dutiable to total Percent	Free	Dutiable [3]/	Total	Ratio of dutiable to total Percent
Animals and animal products, edible	5,750	22,208	27,958	79.4	2,119	12,634	14,754	85.6
Animals and animal products, inedible	56,537	4,625	61,162	7.6	10,010	4,165	14,175	29.4
Vegetable food products and beverages	346,716	188,671	535,388	35.2	174,828	101,172	276,000	36.7
Vegetable products, inedible except fibers and wood	10,106	77,094	87,201	88.4	11,892	33,477	45,369	73.8
Textile fibers and manufactures	24,029	23,579	47,608	49.5	13,116	4,299	17,415	24.7
Wood and paper	690	2,143	2,834	75.6	692	896	1,588	56.4
Nonmetallic minerals	73,293	590	73,883	.9	3,453	16,944	20,397	83.1
Metals and manufactures, except machinery and vehicles	112,021	15,339	127,359	12.0	34,834	3,061	37,895	8.1
Machinery and vehicles	51	45	96	46.8	43	65	108	60.2
Chemicals and related products	40,236	360	40,595	.9	14,150	446	14,596	3.1
Miscellaneous	9,306	737	10,043	7.3	4,788	314	5,101	6.2
Total, all groups	678,736	335,392	1,014,128	33.1	269,924	177,474	447,398	39.7

1/ General imports in 1929.
2/ Preliminary.
3/ Including products subject to import excise taxes.

Source: Compiled from official statistics of the U. S. Department of Commerce.

<u>Tariff status of imports from individual countries</u>. - Imports from many of the Latin American countries are almost entirely duty-free, but from a few they are largely dutiable (see table 20). In 1938 imports from Cuba, chiefly sugar and tobacco, were almost entirely dutiable (though at preferential rates) and those from Argentina, Paraguay, and Uruguay (chiefly canned meats, hides and skins, flaxseed, wool, and quebracho extract), and from Venezuela (chiefly petroleum) were largely dutiable. In general, a larger proportion of the imports from Latin American countries supplying commodities competitive with United States output is dutiable than from countries supplying commodities not produced in this country.

Substantial changes have occurred since 1929 in the ratios of dutiable imports to the total imports coming from Bolivia, Brazil, Venezuela, the Dominican Republic, and Haiti. The shift from the dutiable to duty-free status of most of the imports from Bolivia is due, first, to the contraction of United States imports of dutiable tungsten ore, and, secondly, to the recent increase in imports of antimony ore and refined tin, each of which is duty-free. Dutiable imports from Brazil have increased in relative importance apparently because of the increased United States demand for particular dutiable imports from Brazil, such as canned beef, certain hides and skins, and refined cottonseed oil. The outstanding increase in the dutiable portion of imports from Venezuela has been caused by the import excise tax imposed on petroleum in 1932. The increase in the volume of sugar imported from the Dominican Republic and Haiti accounts for the recent rise in the ratio of dutiable imports from these countries.

Table 20. – United States imports for consumption[1] from
20 Latin American countries: Ratio of dutiable to
total imports, in 1929, 1932, and 1938

Imported from –	1929	1932	1938 [2]
	Percent dutiable		
South America:			
Argentina	62.6	69.4	73.8
Bolivia [3]	91.3	[4]	14.5
Brazil	2.2	2.5	10.2
Chile	2.8	9.6	5.4
Colombia	.4	5.9	.3
Ecuador	15.6	26.7	18.4
Paraguay	74.7	89.0	91.8
Peru	15.4	44.2	22.0
Uruguay	72.2	73.1	90.5
Venezuela	.1	20.6	74.9
Central America:			
Costa Rica	.4	[4]	[4]
El Salvador	5.3	2.1	.9
Guatemala	.6	.2	.4
Honduras	5.7	1.3	1.8
Nicaragua	15.8	2.2	7.6
Panama	7.3	4.0	3.1
Mexico	27.0	31.8	23.9
West Indies:			
Cuba	95.4	91.2	99.2
Dominican Republic	24.9	41.4	41.4
Haiti	9.1	12.8	16.5
Total, all countries –	33.1	28.7	39.7

[1] General imports in 1929 and 1932.
[2] Preliminary.
[3] Imports originating in Bolivia are credited largely to other countries (see table 7).
[4] Less than one-tenth of 1 percent.

Source: Compiled from official statistics of the U. S. Department of Commerce.

<u>United States trade agreements with Latin American countries.</u>

Under the Trade Agreements Act initiated in 1934 and since twice extended
for a 3-year period, the United States has entered into trade agreements
with 21 foreign countries.   Eleven of these are Latin American countries,
namely, Brazil, Colombia, Costa Rica, Cuba, El Salvador, Ecuador,
Guatemala, Haiti, Honduras, Nicaragua,[1] and Venezuela.   The first
agreement negotiated was with Cuba, effective September 3, 1934, and the
most recent was with Venezuela, effective December 16, 1939.

With the exception of imports from Cuba and Venezuela, most of the
imports from Latin American countries with which agreements have been
negotiated thus far consist of duty-free products, and, therefore, the
concessions in many of the agreements have consisted mainly of binding
certain items on the free list.   The leading products so affected were
coffee, bananas, and cacao beans.   The principal imports affected by
reductions in customs duties are sugar (from Cuba), crude petroleum and
fuel oil, Brazil nuts, castor beans, certain types of tobacco (from
Cuba), and pineapples.

<u>United States balance of trade and balance of payments with Latin
America.</u>

The United States customarily has had an import balance of trade
with Latin America as a whole;   only in 1938 and 1939, of the years
1929-39, have United States exports to Latin America exceeded in value
the imports therefrom.[2]   These import trade balances have fluctuated

---

[1] Certain provisions of the agreement with Nicaragua, including the
tariff concessions, were terminated March 10, 1938, at the request of
the Nicaraguan Government.

[2] The export trade balance of the United States with Latin America
in 1938 was 41.3 million dollars;   in 1939 it was 50.9 million dollars.
These export balances, however, would become import balances, if imports
of gold and silver from Latin America were added to imports of merchandise therefrom.

widely. In 1931 the excess of imports from Latin America over exports to that area amounted to 165.5 million dollars, or more than 50 percent of United States exports to that area; in 1930, to 49 million dollars, or about 8 percent of United States exports; and in 1937, to 94 million dollars, or about 16 percent of United States exports. Latin America as a whole is a debtor area, and it is essential that total exports from Latin America (including gold and silver) should exceed total imports into that area if the debt service on obligations due the United States and the returns on United States capital investments are to be paid. Not only must Latin America obtain funds to pay for United States products, to service its debt, and to privide for the remittance of earnings on direct investments of capital; it must also secure funds to pay for shipping and other services regularly purchased from United States citizens (see table 21).

Latin America is assisted in meeting its obligations to this country not only by the sale of goods to the United States and other countries but by the expenditures of United States citizens traveling in Latin American countries (estimated at 68.6 million dollars in 1938), by the disbursements of United States institutions in Latin America (3.3 million dollars), and by the shipment of gold and silver to the United States (149.9 million dollars). In recent years, however, the amounts derived from these sources have been insufficient for all of the remittances due this country.[1]

---

[1] The import or credit side of the Latin American balance of trade is probably overstated by the trade statistics. United States-owned companies in Latin America ship their products to this country and receive in exchange therefor dollar credits. These credits are utilized to pay the expenses of such companies in Latin America and elsewhere. The import trade figures, therefore, will overstate the amount of exchange made available to Latin American countries by the amount of the profits which such companies earn.

The rapid increase of United States exports to Latin America in
the last 4 months of 1939 has made such exports for that year greater
than imports therefrom. Latin America, however, cannot continue indefi-
nitely to take increased quantities of United States goods without
adequate means of payment. The generally accepted means of payment for
imports are gold, silver, credit, and goods and services. Latin
American gold reserves are not adequate to finance any considerable
quantity of United States exports,[1] although the quantity of newly-
mined gold and silver may possibly be increased. An expansion of
exports might be financed through the extension of credits, but this is
only a temporary expedient, since funds must eventually be obtained to
liquidate the increased obligations.

An increase in United States exports to Latin America might also
be financed through an increase in Latin American exports to third
markets, if by this means free exchange could be obtained with which
to pay the United States. But, under existing circumstances, Latin
American exports to third markets may not, in the aggregate, be
increased, and even if they should be, it is doubtful that any increase
in free exchange would be made available to the exporting Latin American
countries, inasmuch as the principal markets for Latin American products
(other than the United States) are European countries which are now
carefully husbanding their supplies of free exchange for the purchase
of essential war materials. If, therefore, the United States would

---

[1] The gold and silver produced in Latin America amount to a considerable sum and have long been used to obtain dollar credits in the
United States. Such gold and silver, however, more nearly resemble
export commodities for these countries.

increase its export trade with Latin America and maintain that
increased trade on a permanent basis, it appears likely that this country must itself provide the means of payment by making it possible for
Latin American countries to sell increased quantities of their products
in the United States market.

Statistics showing the balance of payments between the United
States and Latin America for the years 1929-38 are given in table 21.
These statistics must be interpreted with caution.   Several of the
items are estimates, and statistics for others are not available.
The merchandise trade statistics are unadjusted and include merchandise
for reexport (in both imports and exports), which customarily are
excluded from bilateral statements.[1]

The analysis of a bilateral balance of payments between the United
States and Latin America involves considerations of triangular transactions with third areas, which are not involved when the statement
refers to the transactions of one country with the rest of the world.
For example, the net balance (the last item in the table) may not represent a "disequilibrium" in the balance of payments because this item
represents, in addition to errors and omissions in the statement, a
net balance which may be covered by transactions with other countries.

---

[1] For balance of payments purposes the valuation of certain imports
from Latin America is not altogether satisfactory.   Some commodities,
the output of corporations owned by United States citizens, are imported
at arbitrary invoice values.   Furthermore, the amount of dollar exchange
represented by such shipments may be greater or less than their value as
reported in the official statistics.

Table 21. – Partial balance of payments between the United States and the 20 Latin American countries, 1929-38

(In millions of U. S. dollars)

	1929	1930	1931	1932	1933	1934	1935	1936	1937	1938
Trade and service items:										
Merchandise exports to Latin America 1/	911.8	628.4	312.8	194.4	215.6	307.0	344.1	394.8	578.4	494.8
Merchandise imports from Latin America 1/	1,014.0	677.8	478.3	323.1	316.0	370.9	461.0	501.6	672.5	633.5
Net merchandise exports to (+) or imports (-) from Latin America	-102.2	-49.4	-165.5	-128.5	-100.4	-63.9	-116.9	-106.8	-94.1	-41.3
Receipts from Latin America for shipping services 2/	32.8	22.6	16.3	8.2	4.5	6.4	7.2	8.3	12.1	10.4
Expenditures of Latin American travelers in United States	19.7	24.4	16.8	10.6	9.2	10.4	12.3	14.3	15.2	15.1
Expenditures of United States travelers in Latin America	63.4	82.7	67.2	52.0	40.2	56.8	46.8	61.3	68.7	68.6
Disbursements of United States institutions in Latin America 3/	9.0	8.0	7.2	5.0	3.9	3.4	2.8	2.9	3.2	3.3
Interest receipts from Latin America	87.6	95.5	80.5	46.8	37.3	32.8	35.9	35.5	36.8 4/	14.6
Return on direct investments in Latin America 3/ 5/		120.7	48.0	30.0	10.0	65.0	95.0	131.0	130.0	175.0
Net receipts from Latin America 3/ 5/ for services										
Net receipts from (+) or payments to (-) Latin America on trade and service account	+172.5	+87.2	+38.6	+16.9	+54.4	+100.8	+228.9	+182.2	+143.2	
Gold and silver:										
Net gold imports from Latin America 1/	-89.9	-165.1	-200.7	-51.3	-10.2	-57.8	-42.8	-70.6	-77.9	-101.6
Net silver imports from Latin America 1/	-49.9	-32.9	-20.7	-13.9	-20.1	-24.0	-64.7	-32.0	-31.1	-48.3
Net gold and silver imports from Latin America	-139.8	-198.0	-221.4	-65.2	-30.3	-81.8	-107.5	-102.6	-109.0	-149.9
Capital items:										
Bond-redemption and sinking-fund receipts from Latin America 5/		+39.3	+83.0	+37.0	+19.2	+15.7	(+23.4)	(+32.4)	(+96.9)	(+38.4)
Total reported movement of capital in security transactions 5/ 6/										-3.0
Reported movement of capital in short-term banking funds 7/							+16.0	+15.0	+162.0	-3.0
Reported net exports (+) or imports (-) of paper currency 8/							+55.0	+115.0	+47.0	-18.0
Total reported capital movement 9/	-6.7	-70.0	-31.0	-34.4	+2.6	+1.1	-6.9	-5.5	+2.3	-2.7
		+32.3	+32.0	+22.5	+21.8	+15.8	+6.1	+12.5	+21.3	-21.7
Net balance (based on items listed above) 9/	-104.0–181.0	-42.6	-247.7	-132.5	-62.0	-75.5	-59.5	+44.0	+190.4	+10.9

1/ United States statistics, unadjusted.
2/ Rough estimates.
3/ Not available by countries.
4/ Allowance made for repurchases of Latin American dollar bonds by foreigners.
5/ The data apply to all the West Indies and to Bermuda as well as to the 20 countries specified.
6/ Bond-redemption receipts adjusted for repurchases by foreigners in all years; sinking-fund receipts in 1938 only.
7/ Data compiled by U. S. Treasury.
8/ The data cover movements of U. S. paper currency between the United States and Cuba, Dominican Republic, and Panama.
9/ Inclusive of new investments in Latin America, 1929-34, and of new investments not represented by security issues, 1935-38.
10/ Exclusive of return on U. S. direct investments in Latin America and of all capital transactions except currency movements.

Sources: Especially prepared for this report by the Finance Division, Bureau of Foreign and Domestic Commerce, U. S. Department of Commerce.

SPECIAL PROBLEMS IN THE FOREIGN TRADE OF LATIN AMERICA

Current developments in Latin American trade.

The present European war, if long continued, will doubtless have a marked effect upon the foreign commerce of Latin America. The trade of that area with Europe, already influenced by trade and exchange controls, will likely be further dislocated by the interference of belligerents with commerce and by their demand for certain strategic materials and foodstuffs. The effectiveness of such a demand will depend, of course, upon the ability of the belligerents to export their products to Latin America or to arrange for some other satisfactory method of payment. For the duration of the war, Germany will probably be neither an important market for Latin American products nor an important source of Latin American imports. This will affect certain Latin American countries and commodities more seriously than others. Latin America may cover a part of this loss in trade by increased sales to the United Kingdom and France. But these countries, for financial reasons, will probably confine their purchases, as much as may be, within their own empires.

To the extent that current developments dislocate Latin American trade and restrict the sale of Latin American products, commodity prices and the purchasing power of the people in that area will be depressed. Even if the exports of certain Latin American products to the United Kingdom and France are increased in value, it is not likely that the purchasing power of the Latin American people will be greatly enhanced unless the payment for such exports is made in free exchange, inasmuch as British and French productive capacity will be devoted primarily to the manufacture of those products essential to the prosecution of the war. To the extent that Latin American countries sell their products to the belligerents for blocked currencies, the opportunity for other countries to increase their sales in the markets of Latin America will be materially reduced. In addition to their inability to obtain free exchange, Latin American countries may find an increasing tendency on the part of belligerents to demand payment for goods sold abroad in certain selected foreign currencies; the United Kingdom has recently stipulated that its exports of certain commodities must be paid for only in designated foreign currencies.[1]/

With Germany practically eliminated as a source of Latin American imports, the United Kingdom has an opportunity to regain lost markets, and the United States has an opportunity to increase its already substantial participation in the Latin American import trade. Although the United Kingdom may become a very large purchaser of certain Latin American products, it may, because of its preoccupation with production

---

[1]/ New regulations announced in London on March 9, 1940, reinforced by parallel action in other sterling control countries, are designed to force exporters of specified goods from the sterling control area to certain destinations to require payment either in specified foreign currencies - United States dollars, Swiss francs, Belgian francs, Dutch guilders, or Netherlands Indies guilders - or in sterling purchased with these currencies at the official rates ($4.02½ in the case of the United States dollar). The goods covered by the order issued in London are rubber, tin, jute and jute products, whisky, and furs. An order of the Australian exchange control covers all types of goods exported from Australia. Importers of these goods in the United States will be expected to make payment in their own currency, and importers in all Central and South American countries (excluding British and French possessions, Argentina, and Uruguay) must obtain supplies of one of the specified currencies to finance imports covered by these regulations. Argentina and Uruguay are excepted from the regulations because of the clearing agreements recently concluded between those countries and the countries of the sterling control area. Importers in Argentina and Uruguay must obtain their sterling requirements from the clearing authorities.

for war, be unable to supply the Latin American demand for many commodities. The United States, however, is in a position to fulfill such demands, provided adequate means can be found to finance the trade.

Any attempt to increase United States-Latin American trade must take into account certain basic factors pertinent to the problem. Approximately 60 percent of United States imports (apart from gold and silver) from Latin America consist of raw materials and tropical products which are not produced in the United States, and which enter this market free of duty. Since imports of such products are not curtailed by duties, and since most of them are not restricted by any other type of trade barrier, it appears unlikely that imports of such commodities can be stimulated appreciably except by an increase in their consumption in the United States. Moreover, imports of certain other Latin American products, such as cotton, wheat, corn, barley, oats, and fruits, cannot be greatly increased because for most of these, the United States is itself on an export basis.

If United States exports to Latin America are to be increased, it would appear necessary that United States imports of certain dutiable commodities now obtained from Latin America be increased or that the United States import from Latin America certain products which this country can no longer obtain from customary sources or which it now obtains from sources other than Latin America. Some increase in United States imports of dutiable products may occur as a result of trade agreements concluded with Latin American countries, although such increase is not likely to be large. And the development of new industries in Latin America for the purpose of supplying the United

States market with products hitherto obtained elsewhere will require both time and capital.   Should such a course be pursued, care must be exercised lest the new industries prove unprofitable either because of competition from similar industries in other countries or because of unfavorable local conditions, such as the lack of skilled labor, inadequate power, and unsuitable climate and soil.   To the extent, however, that Latin America becomes a source for products now obtained by the United States from other countries, it is unlikely that United States exports in the aggregate would be increased.

Under more normal conditions it might be expected that increased United States exports to Latin America could be financed through Latin American exports to third countries.   But, because of the piesent war in Europe, it is not likely that the sale of Latin American products in European markets (the principal markets, other than the United States, for Latin American products) will provide any appreciable amount of free exchange which can be utilized by Latin American countries for the purchase of goods from the United States.   Belligerent countries in Europe are safeguarding their dollar exchange for the purchase of war supplies, and it appears improbable that they will permit the utilization of such exchange to finance United States exports to Latin America.

Trade statistics for 1939 and the first 2 months of 1940 indicate that the European war and improved economic conditions in the United States have had an appreciable effect upon United States-Latin American trade (see table 22).   United States imports from Latin America in the first 8 months of 1939 were only 5 percent larger than in the same

period of 1938, and did not increase as rapidly as total United States
imports.   After the outbreak of the European war this situation was
reversed.   United States imports from Latin America in the last 4
months of 1939 were 35 percent greater than in the same 4 months of
1938, while imports from all other countries were only 25 percent
greater.   The rate of increase for imports from Latin America in the
6 months period September to February 1939-40 was less rapid than in
the last 4 months of 1939, and imports from all other countries increased more rapidly.   In the period September to February 1939-40
(the first 6 months of the European war), imports from Latin America
were 32 percent greater than in the corresponding period of 1938-39,
and imports from all other countries were 27 percent greater.

United States exports to Latin America in the first 8 months of
1939 were slightly smaller than in the like period of 1938, but the
decline was not as great as in United States exports to all other
countries.   After the European war began, the trend of United States
exports was altered; total exports increased, and those to Latin
America increased even more rapidly.   In the last 4 months of 1939,
exports to Latin America were 48 percent greater than in the same 4
months of 1938, while exports to all other countries were only 19
percent greater.   The increase in exports to Latin America continued
during the first 2 months of 1940, and exports to all other countries
increased appreciably also.   In the period September to February
1939-40 exports to Latin America were 54 percent greater than in the
same period 1938-39, and exports to all other countries were 33
percent greater.

Table 22. - United States trade with Latin American countries and with all other countries, January - August, and September - December 1938 and 1939, and September - February 1938-39 and 1939-40 1/

(Values in thousands of U.S. dollars)

	January - August			September - December			September - February		
	1938	1939	Percent of change	1938	1939	Percent of change	1938-39	1939-40	Percent of change
General imports									
Latin American countries	312,513	328,038	+5.0	141,004	190,125	+34.8	222,706	293,909	+32.0
All other countries	954,767	1,111,148	+16.4	552,144	688,947	+24.8	806,759	1,026,836	+27.3
General exports 2/									
Latin American countries	331,451	326,698	-1.4	163,371	242,399	+48.4	236,970	364,544	+53.8
All other countries	1,717,661	1,569,624	-8.6	871,957	1,038,623	+19.1	1,229,951	1,631,840	+32.7

1/ Preliminary.
2/ Includes reexports.

Source: Compiled from official statistics of the U.S. Department of Commerce.

Comparison of Latin American and United States trade, 1913-19.

Although the United States was able to increase its share of the
import trade of Latin America, both absolutely and relatively, during
the period 1914-18, it should not be assumed that the course of Latin
American trade during the present war can be accurately predicted on
the basis of that experience.   In fact, developments in United States-
Latin American trade resulting from the present European war may be
very different from those of the last war.   Nevertheless, it may be
useful to examine the trend of Latin American trade with the world and
with the United States during the period of the World War, 1914-18.

As a result of the World War, the foreign trade of Latin America
experienced a marked expansion.   In the 7 years 1913-19, exports increased 100 percent, in terms of value, and imports nearly 50 percent.
Substantial as was this rise in the foreign trade of Latin America, it
was exceeded by the growth of the total foreign trade of the United
States.   United States exports to the world were valued at 200 percent
more in 1919 than in 1913, and imports were valued at 100 percent more.
The larger relative increase in the trade of the United States may be
attributed to a number of factors.   For the duration of the war, the
United States supplied certain of the belligerents with essential commodities.   During a part of the period 1913-19, the United States was
itself participating in the war;   the resulting stimulation of production and the increased demand for raw materials brought about a
sharp rise in the quantity and value of imported products.   United
States loans to the Allies, both before and after this country became
a participant in the hostilities, were used almost entirely to purchase

essential war supplies (including foodstuffs) in the United States,
and thus served to stimulate United States exports.   In addition to
the exports of raw materials, such as wheat, cotton, copper, and
petroleum, by the United States, its productive plant capacity enabled
it to meet the demand of European countries for manufactured war
materials which could not be supplied elsewhere.   Moreover, the United
States had an advantage in shipping facilities and in its proximity to
important European markets.   A comparison of the trends of the foreign
trade of the United States and Latin America during the period 1913-19
is presented in table 23.

Table 23. - Comparison of United States exports and imports with those of Latin America, 1913-19

(Values in thousands of U.S. dollars)

Year 1/	Exports		Imports	
	Latin America	United States 2/	Latin America	United States 3/
1913	1,547,989	2,465,884	1,326,640	1,813,008
1914	1,274,997	2,364,579	907,841	1,893,926
1915	1,658,469	2,768,589	809,926	1,674,170
1916	1,866,967	4,333,483	1,040,662	2,107,884
1917	2,062,424	6,290,048	1,367,239	2,659,355
1918	2,408,444	5,919,711	1,549,685	2,945,655
1919	3,103,406	7,920,426	1,949,367	3,904,365
Percent increase, 1919 compared with 1913	100.5	221.2	46.9	115.4

1/ Latin American trade reported in calendar years, United States trade reported in fiscal years ended June 30, except 1919, which was on a calendar year basis.
2/ Includes reexports.
3/ General imports.

Source: Latin American trade - A Statistical Account of the Foreign Trade of Latin America Before and During the World War (tabulated by Pan American Union). United States trade - Foreign Commerce and Navigation of the United States.

Latin American trade, 1913-19.

Exports. - The export trade of Latin America was greatly affected by the World War. In general, prices of the principal export products of that area increased and in many instances, the quantities exported increased also, especially of those products essential to the prosecution of the war, such as tin, copper, wheat, cotton, meats, wool, and hides and skins. This rise in the value and volume of

exports from Latin America, however, did not follow immediately after
the declaration of war.   In fact, exports were smaller in terms of
value in 1914 than in 1913.   This decline was a reflection of the
adverse economic conditions which prevailed in 1914 and which were
intensified by the dislocation of markets and trade routes, and the
inadequacy of shipping facilities following the declaration of war.
These conditions operated to reduce the prices of many export products
and thus to reduce the value, as well as the volume, of exports.   Exports in 1915 increased, exceeding those in 1913, and thereafter they
increased each year until in 1919 they were 100 percent greater, in
terms of value, than they had been the year before the war began. [1/]

The extent to which the export trade of the individual Latin
American countries was affected by the war was dependent principally
upon the character of their export products and the war demand for
them.   During the war the prices of certain essential minerals, foodstuffs, and other agricultural products doubled and even trebled,
whereas the prices of such commodities as coffee and cacao beans
remained fairly stable until immediately after the Armistice.   This
situation is reflected in the export trade of individual Latin American
countries.   Nearly all of these countries felt the adverse impact of
the war in 1914 and their exports in that year declined as compared
with exports in 1913.   After 1914, however, there was no such marked
uniformity in trade trends.

[1/] See table 24 for prices, and table 25 for trend of exports.

The export trade of Bolivia which then, as now, consisted chiefly of minerals, especially tin, rose sharply after 1914, and reached a peak in 1918, the last year of the war. In 1918 Bolivian exports were nearly 100 percent larger than they were in 1913. In 1919, however, Bolivian exports declined sharply. The export trade of Chile, principally copper and nitrates, followed an almost identical pattern. The minerals which these countries supplied were in great demand while the war was being prosecuted, but with its termination that demand was abruptly curtailed and their export trade declined.

Exports from Argentina followed a different trend. Although they increased after 1914, the rate of increase was not marked in the years 1915-17. In 1918, however, exports rose sharply and continued their upward trend in 1919 after peace had been restored. The principal Argentine export products in those years were wheat, corn, flaxseed, meats, wool, hides and skins, and quebracho. Most of these products are important from the standpoint of a wartime economy, and hence were in demand in Europe. The entry of the United States into the war, improved transportation facilities, and rapidly rising prices (1917-19) probably accounted for the marked increase in Argentine exports in 1918-19, although the tremendous demand for food in Europe after the Armistice was doubtless a further factor contributing to the rise.

Brazilian exports after 1914 remained relatively stable and did not exceed their 1913 value until 1919. Coffee and cacao were not considered essential war commodities and the price of those products which accounted for the major portion of Brazilian exports, did not increase appreciably until 1919, when they rose nearly 100 percent

above the average of the year before. Europe, which had long been
denied such products, was free once again to gratify its taste for
these beverages, and Brazilian exports rose from 284 million dollars
in 1918 to 571 million dollars in 1919. Exports from Colombia and
Venezuela, then principally coffee and cacao, followed similar trends.

Exports from Cuba increased each year during the period 1913-19.
The increases were especially marked in 1916, when exports rose 100
million dollars over those in 1915, and in 1919, when they rose 160
million dollars over those in 1918. These increases coincided with
sharp advances in the price of sugar, which has long constituted a
very large proportion of total Cuban exports. Indeed, the increase
in Cuban exports is attributable principally to the rise in sugar
prices and to the increase in the volume of sugar exports caused in
part by the decline in the production of beet sugar in Europe during
the war.

Total Latin American exports to the United States increased each
year during the period 1913-19; in 1913 they amounted to 481 million
dollars, and in 1919 to 1,389 million dollars, an increase of 190
percent. Moreover, the United States took an increasing share of
Latin American products. In 1913, 31 percent of Latin American exports went to the United States; in 1917, 51 percent, and in 1919,
45 percent (see table 26).

Nearly all of the Latin American countries increased their
exports to the United States during this period; notable among these
were Argentina, Bolivia, Ecuador, Paraguay, Peru, Uruguay, and Cuba,
the Dominican Republic, and Haiti. Exports from Chile to the United

States declined sharply in 1919, as did those from Bolivia (though to
a lesser extent), because of price reductions and lessened demand for
their principal export products - nitrates, copper, and tin. Brazilian exports to the United States and exports from Venezuela, however,
increased markedly (in terms of value) in 1919 because the cessation
of war made possible a greater consumption of coffee and cacao in
Europe, and the prices of these products rose in that year. Exports
from the West Indian republics increased steadily throughout the entire
period 1913-19, but had their greatest rise in 1919 when the price of
sugar advanced sharply.

Table 24. - Prices of commodities important in Latin American export trade, 1913-19

Product	Unit	1913	1914	1915	1916	1917	1918	1919
Minerals:								
Copper, electrolytic 1/ ————	Cents per lb.	15.5	2/ 13.6	17.3	27.2	27.2	3/ 24.6	3/ 18.7
Manganese ore 4/ ————	Dollars per ton 5/	5/	5/	15.83	25.00	48.33	63.62	33.06
Petroleum, crude 6/ ————	Dollars per bbl.	0.94	0.78	0.58	1.20	1.73	2.23	2 20
Tin ————	Cents per lb.	44.3	35.8	38.6	43.4	61.9	85.3	65.7
Pastoral products:								
Cattle hides 7/ —————	Cents per lb.	19.7	19.4	22.6	26.9	33.4	30.9	38.2
Wool, raw 8/ —————	Cents per lb.	36.8	28.3	37.1	44.2	72.0	80.3	80.8
Lamb 9/ —————	Cents per lb.	12.7	13.5	16.1	19.3	20.8	26.2	22.3
Beef 10/ —————	Cents per lb.	8.6	10.7	14.4	16.8	22.0	22.3	22 5
Agricultural products:								
Barley 11/ —————	Dollars per bu.	0.65	0.72	0.69	1.19	1.46	1.04	1.45
Cacao beans 12/ —————	Cents per lb.	15.3	13.0	17.6	17.0	12.9	13.6	22.5
Coffee 13/ —————	Cents per lb.	11.1	8.2	7.5	9.2	9.3	9.4	17.9
Corn 14/ —————	Dollars per bu.	0.70	0.70	0.79	1.11	1.63	1.62	1.59
Cotton, Brazilian fair 15/ —.	Cents per lb.	15.0	11.6	16.1	25.9	47.8	46.9	48.4
Cotton, Peruvian good 15/ ——:	Cents per lb.	16.3	12.4	16.6	26 8	50.1	49.7	62.1
Flaxseed 16/ —————	Dollars per bu.	1.21	1.26	1.12	1.58	2.40	2.56	5/
Henequen 17/ —————	Cents per lb.	4.3	5.1	5.9	9.0	17.7	17.8	13.3
Oats 18/ —————	Cents per bu.	40.0	50.0	41.0	54.0	71.0	70.0	80.0
Sugar 19/ —————	Cents per lb.	2.0	2.6	3.3	4.4	4.6	4.2	5.1
Wheat 20/ —————	Dollars per bu.	1.06	1.57	1.75	2.24	2.35	2.40	2.15
Chemical products:								
Quebracho extract (solid) 21/ .	Cents per lb.	4.8	5.0	5.0	15.0	15.0	13.5	9.8
Sodium nitrate 22/ —————	Cents per lb.	2.5	2.1	2.4	3.2	4 0	4.7	3.6

1/ Source, Engineering and Mining Journal.   2/ 9 months average.   3/ 11 months average.
4/ C i f. North Atlantic ports on basis of 50 percent ore.   Sources, Iron Trade Review.
5/ Not available.
6/ Prices at wells in Kansas-Oklahoma.   Source, Geological Survey and U S. Bureau of Mines.
7/ Buenos Aires frigorifics steers at New York.   Source, Pratt's Daily Reports on Hides and Skins.
8/ Prices for Montivideo crossbred choice wool in the grease at Boston.   Source, Bulletins of the National Association of Wool Manufacturers.
9/ Prices for New Zealand first quality lambs at London.   Source, Cattle and Beef Survey, U.S. Tariff Commission.
10/ Prices for Argentine first quality chilled beef at London.   Source, Cattle and Beef Survey, U.S. Tariff Commission.
11/ Chicago prices.   Source, Agricultural Statistics.
12/ Prices for Arriba at New York.   Source, Wholesale Price Bulletin 1927; U.S. Department of Labor.
13/ Prices for Rio No. 7 at New York.   Source, Wholesale Price Bulletin 1927, U S. Department of Labor.
14/ Prices for No 3 yellow at New York   Source, Agricultural Yearbook 1928.
15/ Spot prices at Liverpool for crop year beginning August 1.   Source, Statistics on Cotton and Related Data, December 1939, U.S. Department of Agriculture.
16/ Prices at Buenos Aires.   Source, International Price Comparisons, 1919, U S. Department of Commerce.
17/ Average wholesale price at New York.   Source, Compiled from War Trade Bulletin No. 32, Cordage Trade Journal, and New York Journal of Commerce.
18/ Prices for No. 3 white at Chicago, Source, Agricultural Yearbook 1924.
19/ Prices are official Cuban promedio.   Source, Statistics on Sugar, 1939, U.S. Tariff Commission.
20/ Prices are for imported wheat at Liverpool   Source, Agricultural Statistics, 1939.
21/ Source, Bureau of Labor Statistics.
22/ Source, Oil, Paint and Drug Reporter.

Table 25. - Latin America: Total exports of the 20 Latin American countries, 1913-19

(Value in thousands of U.S. dollars)

Country	1913	1914	1915	1916	1917	1918	1919
Total, 20 Latin American countries	1,547,989	1,274,997	1,658,469	1,866,967	2,062,424	2,408,444	3,103,406
South America:							
Argentina	468,999	338,777	541,532	527,045	533,665	777,358	1,000,036
Bolivia	36,551	25,662	37,132	39,579	61,522	71,219	56,258
Brazil	315,165	221,539	257,177	272,853	306,389	284,275	570,943
Chile	144,653	109,382	119,530	187,458	259,985	291,863	115,697
Colombia	34,316	32,633	31,579	31,654	31,893	37,729	76,917
Ecuador	15,789	13,062	12,895	17,570	16,309	13,365	21,005
Paraguay	5,462	4,447	8,624	8,190	11,364	11,058	14,372
Peru	44,410	42,611	68,638	80,390	90,607	97,067	130,731
Uruguay	65,142	54,516	76,222	71,074	96,217	120,249	153,182
Venezuela	29,484	21,521	23,404	22,707	23,165	19,813	49,923
Central America:							
Costa Rica	10,433	10,979	9,972	11,121	11,382	9,624	17,749
El Salvador	9,929	10,796	10,564	11,605	16,050	17,360	16,745
Guatemala	14,450	12,754	11,567	10,638	7,810	11,319	22,419
Honduras	3,300	3,421	3,142	4,191	8,030	5,734	5,998
Nicaragua	7,712	4,955	4,567	5,285	5,975	7,755	12,409
Panama	5,383	3,801	3,423	5,507	5,624	2,900	3,757
Mexico	150,203 :1/	165,000 :1/	156,000 :1/	170,000 :1/	180,000 :1/	187,784 :2/	198,234
West Indies:							
Cuba	164,823	177,554	254,292	356,571	366,772	413,325	575,968
Dominican Republic	10,470	10,589	15,209	21,528	22,445	22,372	39,602
Haiti	11,316 :1/	11,000 :1/	13,000 :1/	12,000	7,220	6,276	21,460

1/ Estimated.
2/ Compiled from Mexican Statistics (1929 annual). Exchange rates: 1918, $0.50; 1919, $0.5034 (Commerce Yearbook).

Source: A Statistical Account of the Foreign Trade of Latin America Before and During the World War, Pan American Union, 1919.

Table 26. - Latin America: Exports of the 20 Latin American countries to the United States, 1913-19

(Value in thousands of U.S. dollars)

Country	1913	1914	1915	1916	1917	1918	1919
Total, 20 Latin American countries	481,127 1/	486,835	667,565	868,433	1,061,701	1,126,682	1,389,293
Percent of total exports	31.1	38.2	40.3	46.5	51.5	46.9	44.8
South America:							
Argentina	22,208	41,581	87,148	110,064	156,433	160,147	185,007
Bolivia	218	956	9,757	11,269	22,193	29,637	23,237
Brazil	102,563	92,096	107,524	124,920	134,131	98,474	234,461
Chile	30,413	31,434	50,199	92,034	154,943	178,483	47,623
Colombia	18,862	18,272	21,946	27,294 1/	26,000	31,134 1/	54,000
Ecuador	3,834	3,588	5,678	8,585	12,772	10,429	10,100
Paraguay	-	13	465	414	359	904	625
Peru	14,742	14,808	31,057	50,565	53,180	45,193	60,746
Uruguay	2,972	9,597	12,217	17,554	26,219	24,174	44,603
Venezuela	8,476	9,379	13,170	11,796	12,793	8,889	23,642
Central America:							
Costa Rica	5,297	4,894	4,865	6,831	8,119	8,706	9,812
El Salvador	2,824	2,662	3,716	4,102	10,043	14,766	8,340
Guatemala	3,923	4,874	6,881	8,669 1/	7,600 1/	8,100	19,187
Honduras	2,869	2,974	3,041 1/	4,000	7,679	5,429	5,542
Nicaragua	2,722	2,428	3,080	3,731	5,092	6,413	7,664
Panama	4,802	3,270	3,119	5,361	5,528	2,846	3,493
Mexico	116,018 1/	86,000 1/	84,000 1/	110,000 1/	140,000 1/	175,037	176,565
West Indies:							
Cuba	131,784	148,264	206,164	250,090	257,373	294,665	441,057
Dominican Republic	5,601 1/	8,573	12,044	17,412	17,947	18,170	24,040
Haiti	1,000 1/	1,172 1/	1,495 1/	3,745 1/	3,297	5,086	9,546

1/ Estimated.

Source: A Statistical Account of the Foreign Trade of Latin America Before and During the World War, Pan American Union, 1919.

Imports. - Imports into Latin America in the period 1913-19 increased less rapidly than did exports therefrom; moreover, the rise
in imports had its inception at a later date.   Imports, which were
valued at 1.3 billion dollars in 1913, declined sharply in 1914 and
in 1915.   Not until 1917 did they regain their former level.   By
1919, however, imports amounted to over 1.9 billion dollars, an
increase of nearly 50 percent over those in 1913 (see table 27).
The early decline was due in part to the inability of Latin American
countries to obtain goods from Germany and Austria-Hungary, and to
obtain certain types of goods from the other belligerents.   Moreover, established trade routes and sailing schedules were severly
dislocated during the war, and there was an acute shortage of
shipping facilities.   Later, Latin American countries purchased a
larger proportion of their imports from the United States.   The increase in prices also contributed to the rise in the value of Latin
American imports.

The import trade of each of the 20 Latin American countries,
except Uruguay and Costa Rica, was larger in 1919 than in 1913.   In
most instances the trade declined during the period 1913-15 and increased thereafter.   Imports into Argentina and Uruguay, however, did
not begin to rise until 1917, whereas the trade of Cuba began to increase in 1915.   This divergence in trade trends may be explained by
the difference in the trend and composition of the exports of these

countries and the effect of such exports upon purchasing power.[1]
Imports into all of the Latin American countries, except Chile and
Mexico, were larger in 1919 after the war was over than they had been
in the previous year.   The decline in Chilean and Mexican imports
in 1919 was probably caused in part by the cessation of the demand
and the decline in the prices for their mineral products following
the termination of hostilities.

Latin American imports from the United States declined from 328
million dollars in 1913 to 254 million dollars in 1914; thereafter
they increased until they amounted to 1,020 million dollars in 1919,
an increase above the 1913 level of more than 200 percent (see table
28).   Moreover, the share of the United States in Latin American
import trade rose from 25 percent in 1913 to 50 percent in the years
1916-19.   United States participation reached a peak of 56 percent
in 1917; the next year, when the United States was fully engaged in
the war, its participation declined to 53 percent, and in 1919 to
52 percent.   Peace had been restored in 1919 and European countries
were free once more to engage in foreign trade, though they did not
immediately regain their former place in the Latin American market.

Imports into all of the Latin American countries from the United
States were greater in 1919 than in 1913; and all of these countries,

---

[1] Argentina and Uruguay exported principally animal products and
cereals, and Cuba chiefly sugar.   Exports from the first two countries
did not increase appreciably until 1918-19, while Cuban exports rose
throughout the entire period.

except Chile and Mexico, made larger dollar purchases from the
United States in 1919 than in the previous year. This rise in the
value of Latin American imports from the United States was due to
increases both in quantities and in prices, especially prices.

Table 27. - Latin America: Total imports of the 20 Latin American countries, 1913-19

(Value in thousands of U.S. dollars)

Country	1913	1914	1915	1916	1917	1918	1919
Total, 20 Latin American countries	1,326,640	907,841	809,926	1,040,662	1,367,239	1,549,685	1,949,367
South America:							
Argentina	408,712	263,663	220,086	210,887	368,912	485,582	636,099
Bolivia	21,358	15,507	8,804	12,128	13,058	13,601	24,179
Brazil	326,429	165,747	146,082	194,582	215,299	247,351	349,648
Chile	120,274	98,461	55,922	81,220	129,603	159,167	146,483
Colombia	28,536	20,979	17,840	29,660	26,098	22,034	46,194
Ecuador	8,837	8,403	8,408	9,330	10,177	8,112	11,668
Paraguay	7,876	4,995	2,334	4,559	8,902	10,720	15,361
Peru	29,591	23,464	15,044	42,200	65,624	47,167	59,311
Uruguay	50,666	38,724	36,379	35,155	38,701	39,822	43,788
Venezuela	18,030	13,987	13,470	21,292	22,188	15,434	35,904
Central America:							
Costa Rica	8,778	7,633	4,479	6,604	5,595	3,735	7,518
El Salvador	6,174	4,959	4,022	5,824	6,896	6,143	14,958
Guatemala	10,062	9,331	5,072	8,539	8,992	6,634	14,216
Honduras	5,133	6,625	5,874	4,452	6,293	4,784	6,931
Nicaragua	5,770	4,134	3,159	4,778	6,393	5,930	7,913
Panama	11,397	9,885	9,037	9,197	9,223	7,822	11,407
Mexico	97,886 1/	78,000 1/	85,000 1/	90,000 1/	128,000 1/	138,108 2/	119,325
West Indies:							
Cuba	143,759	119,001	155,448	248,278	271,280	297,622	359,327
Dominican Republic	9,272	6,729	9,119	11,664	17,400	19,736	22,019
Haiti	8,100	7,613	4,345	10,312	8,606	10,181	17,118

1/ Estimated.
2/ Compiled from Mexican statistics (1929 annual). Exchange rates - 1918, $0.50; 1919, $0.5034 (Commerce Yearbook).

Source: A Statistical Account of the Foreign Trade of Latin America Before and During the World War, Pan American Union, 1919.

Table 28. — Latin America: Imports of the 20 Latin American countries from the United States, 1913-19

(Value in thousands of U.S. dollars)

Country	1913	1914	1915	1916	1917	1918	1919
Total, 20 Latin American countries	327,589	253,596	337,519	538,064	769,656	792,384	1,019,633
Percent of total imports	24.7	27.9	41.7	51.7	56.3	53.1	52.3
South America:							
Argentina	60,172	35,584	54,474	61,626	133,942	164,415	225,815
Bolivia	1,577	1,808	1,859	3,664	4,355	4,411	5,804
Brazil	51,290	30,075	46,858	76,239	101,092	88,983	146,048
Chile	20,089	20,149	18,638	34,459	63,535	74,260	70,027
Colombia	7,630	6,487	8,662	15,098 1/	14,700	11,370 1/	28,000
Ecuador	2,818	2,771	3,204	5,354	5,932	4,633	8,171
Paraguay	474	416	273	847	1,516	1,763	2,632
Peru	8,531	7,634	7,233	24,867	42,733	25,606	36,691
Uruguay	6,637 1/	4,150	7,562	9,262	11,009	9,510	15,571
Venezuela	6,944	6,015	7,943	12,959	15,562	8,867	25,623
Central America:							
Costa Rica	4,516	4,022	3,032	4,677	3,888	2,162	5,891
El Salvador	2,491	2,028	2,474	3,587	4,260	3,455	9,064
Guatemala	5,053	4,879	3,752	6,535 1/	7,200 1/	6,118	10,213
Honduras	3,457	5,262	5,177	4,085	5,795	4,358 1/	6,500
Nicaragua	3,244	2,566	2,593	3,856	5,171	4,630	6,688
Panama	6,379	6,396	6,822	6,675	7,063	6,351	9,359
Mexico	48,644 1/	33,216 1/	41,071 1/	60,000 1/	115,000 1/	123,769	100,280
West Indies:							
Cuba	75,968	69,305	104,723	185,337	205,104	222,262	273,202
Dominican Republic	5,769	4,452	7,361	10,163	14,320	17,037	18,113
Haiti	5,909	6,382	3,807	8,775	7,478	9,423	15,940

1/ Estimated.

Source: A Statistical Account of the Foreign Trade of Latin America Before and During the World War, Pan American Union, 1919.

Changes in economic conditions between 1914 and 1939.

Far-reaching changes in world economy and trade have taken place since 1914-18. The trade of Latin American countries with the world and with the United States, in terms of value, declined abruptly in 1921 and 1922, and has not since regained the levels attained in 1919-20, although it increased irregularly during the period 1923-29. The trade of most other countries, including that of the United States, followed a similar trend. Changes other than those in trade have also occurred. The economic organization of the main geographic areas of the world and of the individual countries within these areas has been greatly altered. This has affected the foreign trade of the United States, and will doubtless further affect the trade of this country with Latin America during the period of armed conflict.

The economy of the United States has changed materially since 1914. New industrial and agricultural capacities have been developed. This country is now a creditor rather than a debtor nation. It has also accumulated a large part of the world's gold supply. The possibility of an expansion in United States trade, such as occurred in 1914-18 with Latin American and other countries, is problematical. The future course of the trade of the United States will be affected by the changes which have occurred since 1914 in the ability of the United States and of other countries to supply their own needs, by the tariff and credit policies of the United States, and by the ability of Latin American countries to maintain their export markets and to obtain free exchange for the products which they sell.

When hostilities began in 1914, the United Kingdom was the center
of world commerce. With its credits, commercial services, and
trading contacts it provided the most important medium through which
raw materials from relatively undeveloped areas moved into world
consumption, and from which such areas obtained their supplies of
manufactured goods. To a lesser extent, Belgium, France, Germany,
and Italy performed similar functions in the international economy.
Dislocations arising from the war in 1914-18 caused the center of
economic activity to shift from Europe, and the United States gradually
took over a substantial part of the services in international trade
and finance previously performed by the European countries. Moreover, new trading facilities were developed, making possible a
direct interchange between the United States and other raw material
producing countries.

Probably more important than commercial changes in affecting
the movement of goods have been agricultural and industrial developments which have altered the surplus and deficit positions of
individual countries with respect to various types of goods. The
most striking of these changes has been the industrial expansion of
Japan and the Soviet Union, and the agricultural expansion in Germany
and Italy. In Latin America, many countries have also attempted to
diversify their agriculture and to stimulate their industries. The
move toward self-sufficiency in both agriculture and industry has
been widespread. It has led not only to the creation of new supplies
within various countries, but also to the encouragement of similar

developments within political spheres of influence, such as the
British, French, and Netherlands empires, and within economic spheres
of influence such as those created by Germany, Italy, and Japan.

The effect of these changes is strikingly illustrated by the
shift in the importance of the main geographic areas as sources of
United States imports and as markets for United States exports.   In
1914, Europe supplied about 47 percent of all United States imports;
Latin America, 25 percent; Asia, 15 percent; and northern North
America (principally Canada and Newfoundland), 9 percent.   In 1938,
Europe supplied approximately 29 percent of all United States imports;
Asia, 25 percent; Latin America, 23 percent; and northern North
America, 14 percent.   There has been a somewhat similar change in
the markets for United States exports.   In 1914, Europe absorbed
63 percent of all United States exports; northern North America,
15 percent; Latin America, 12 percent; and Asia, 5 percent.   In
1938, Europe took approximately 40 percent of United States shipments abroad; Asia about 17 percent; Latin America, 16 percent;
and northern North America, 15 percent.

Shifts in the importance of countries in the trade of the United
States have not only resulted from changes in trading and credit
facilities and in productive capacities, but also, especially since
1930, from government policies influencing consumption requirements
and the means of supplying them.   These have taken the form of
trade controls which have affected not only the country adopting
such controls, but also the countries engaging in trade with the

country adopting them.   In contrast to the relatively free markets
of 25 years ago (except for customs duties), a large fraction of the
world's trade now flows through channels created by the policies of
governments - policies which have brought about the imposition of
such restrictive measures as quotas, exchange controls, and clearing
and barter agreements.   These policies, especially because they
affect foreign exchange and credit facilities, introduce serious
obstacles to the movement of international commerce.   The situation
is especially important in South American, and certain European and
Asiatic countries in which intergovernmental agreements and policies
have exercised a strong influence on the movements of trade.

Influences of the war on world economy.

In still other ways present conditions differ from those in 1914.
The scarcity of raw materials during the last World War was caused in
large part by the absence of adequate controls early in the conflict.
The failure to conserve and to plan for the efficient utilization of
agricultural and industrial resources led to waste and ultimate
scarcity.   Indeed, there was little or no control, even over foreign
exchange, until near the end of the conflict.   But in the present
war, European countries began with a severe regimentation of their
economic life, if they had not already undertaken it before the war.
Efforts are being made to curtail the consumption of basic foodstuffs
and raw materials, and this should operate to restrict the demand
for the imports of those commodities.

A second factor which should operate to lessen the demand for goods during the present war, as compared with the last one, is the extent to which the economies of the belligerent countries were transformed to meet military requirements prior to the present war's inception. It is the transfer of industrial capacity from production for civilian consumption to production for war purposes that provides a major impetus to the increased consumption of industrial and certain other raw materials; but a very large part of the industrial capacity of the belligerent nations had already been shifted to wartime production before the war began. One of the principal factors making for an increased demand in times of war, therefore, has been operative for some time and is not likely to be economically so effective as it was in 1914-18. In fact, it appears probable that the rate of increase will be slower and the absolute increase in the demand for many commodities will be smaller than it was during the last war.

The demand for commodities is likely to be lessened not only as a result of governmental activity, planning, and control, but also because the purchasing power of the belligerents is appreciably smaller than it was in 1914. It is reported that British and French reserves of gold, dollar exchange, and foreign securities at the inception of the present war aggregated approximately 7 billion dollars, but these reserves are the equivalent of only a small part of the funds expended in foreign markets by the European belligerents during the last war including those funds made available by United States loans. At that time, in addition to the very large reserves

maintained abroad by the United Kingdom and France, both Germany
and Austria-Hungary had substantial balances in foreign countries.
Moreover, Germany, as well as the United Kingdom and France, owned
valuable assets in foreign countries, other than gold, exchange, and
securities, and some of these were liquidated in order to finance
the purchase of essential war materials. Such assets are not now
available to the extent they were in 1914. Furthermore, neutral
countries, especially the United States, made large credits available
to belligerent nations during the last war, but similar credits
either are not now being extended, or if extended, are being granted
on a more restricted basis.

In 1939 the world production of practically all of the basic
raw materials was very much greater than in 1914. This is true of
such products as oil, steel, copper, cotton, wool, sugar, and grain.
If the present European war continues for any considerable period of
time, it will operate to increase the prices of most of these
commodities. Indeed, the prices of some basic commodities have
already advanced somewhat, but it appears improbable that a sharp
and sustained rise in prices resulting from a scarcity of essential
raw materials will develop in the very near future. Such a scarcity
is unlikely not only because minor increases in prices will stimulate
new production, but also because existing productive capacity is
adequate to meet a very substantial increase in demand. All of these
factors will have their influence upon the trade of Latin America
with the world and with the United States.

Effects of the war on the foreign trade of Latin America.

Thus far the most direct and obvious impact of the war on Latin American trade has been the practical elimination of Germany as a consumer of Latin American products and as a supplier of a wide range of consumption and capital goods.[1] It is also probable that Latin American trade with other European countries will be considerably affected by the war. The demands of belligerent countries for goods, together with the diversion of men from certain industrial pursuits to military service, will operate to reduce exports of all European countries to Latin America and to other overseas areas. Similarly, there will be a tendency for imports of some Latin American products by Great Britain, France, and the neutral European countries to be curtailed. Italy, for financial reasons, may restrict its imports of certain Latin American goods, and other European countries, through government controls or otherwise, may be less important markets for some Latin American commodities than they formerly were. Furthermore, it is likely that the United Kingdom and France will attempt to obtain increased proportions of their imports from within their empires, and from countries in the sterling bloc. A shortage of vessels, and interference with shipping and the rationing of essential commodities by the Allies may also operate to reduce European markets for Latin American products.

---

[1] Other markets and sources of supply which have been largely, if not completely, eliminated as factors in Latin American trade because of absorption by Germany, are Austria, Czechoslovakia, Poland, and Denmark. Norway, Sweden, and Finland will doubtless become less important in Latin American trade for the duration of the war.

The net effects of the war on the export trade of Latin America
with European countries other than Germany, however, are very uncertain. It is likely that European consumption of products such as
meats and wool, as well as of petroleum and copper, may be increased,
and that the United Kingdom and France, even if they make a serious
attempt to do so, will be unable to obtain from within their empires
larger quantities of certain commodities which they have been importing from Latin America.[1] Moreover, to the extent that Germany
draws more heavily than formerly on the countries of south and
eastern Europe for agricultural products, other western European
nations will be forced to place greater dependence than before on
overseas sources, including Latin America. Furthermore, increases
in prices resulting from war demands, especially for such products as
copper, petroleum, and wool, may tend to raise the value of Latin
American exports to European and other countries.

The trade of the 20 Latin American republics, and the portions
thereof accounted for by the United States, the United Kingdom,
Germany, Japan, Italy, and France, in specified years, 1929 to 1938,
is shown in table 6. Further analysis of the trade statistics of
the 20 Latin American republics indicates that in 1937 about 45
percent of the exports to countries other than those shown separately
in table 6 (amounting to about 350 million dollars, or about 15

---

[1] Since the outbreak of the war, the United Kingdom has made
substantial purchases of beef in Argentina. It is impossible at this
time to determine whether these purchases presage continued heavy
demands by the United Kingdom for Argentine beef for the duration of
the war.

percent of total Latin American exports in that year) went to other
European countries, of which the most important was Belgium.   The
Netherlands, Sweden, and other countries accounted for lesser amounts.
An equal or somewhat greater value of exports was accounted for by
the trade of the 20 Latin American countries with one another and
with other countries in the Western Hemisphere.   Of the latter
trade, exports of crude petroleum, principally from Venezuela to the
Netherlands West Indies, were valued at about 200 million dollars.
Most of the petroleum moving in this trade is subsequently shipped in
the form of refined products to other countries, the United States
and the United Kingdom being the principal markets.   The exports of
these refined products are not covered by the tables here given,
since these tables do not show the trade of the territories in South
and Central America belonging to overseas countries.   If this trade
were included, the figures for Latin American products taken by the
United States and European countries, especially the United Kingdom,
would be larger than shown in the tables.   Exports of Latin American
products to Canada were valued at about 39 million dollars in 1937.

Approximately 14 percent of the total imports of Latin American
countries in 1937 (amounting to about 225 million dollars) came from
European countries other than those shown separately in table 6;
about 12 percent (amounting to about 182 million dollars) consisted of
trade of the Latin American republics with one another.

Table 29 shows the exports and imports of the 20 Latin American republics in 1937 approximately as they were distributed among the areas just referred to, as well as among the six countries covered separately in table 6.   The figures are only approximate because of the deficiencies and inaccuracies of the statistics.   In any case, no importance attaches to the precise figures since the relative position of the different countries and areas in the trade changes considerably from one year to another.   The table may be regarded only as indicative of the approximate distribution of Latin American trade before the present war.

Table 29. – Latin America: Approximate distribution
of the trade of the 20 Latin American
countries to various markets, 1937

(Value in millions of U.S. dollars)

Country	Exports		Imports	
	Value	Percent of total	Value	Percent of total
Total, all countries	2,323	100.0	1,616	100.0
UNITED STATES	719	31.0	551	34.1
Canada	39	1.7	18	1.1
Netherlands West Indies	200	8.6		
Other countries in the Western Hemisphere 1/	140	6.0	2/ 182	10.8
United Kingdom	408	17.6	213	13.2
Germany	203	8.7	250	15.4
France	94	4.0	48	3.0
Italy	70	3.0	38	2.3
Other countries in Europe	349	15.0	226	14.0
Japan	38	1.6	46	2.9
Other countries in Asia, Africa and Oceania	16	.7	48	3.0
Not reported by country	3/ 47	2.0		

1/ Principally the Latin American countries themselves.
2/ Includes small imports from the Netherlands West Indies.
3/ Consists principally of exports of sodium nitrate and iodine
from Chile, not reported separately, but for which the United States
is much the largest customer. Egypt, Germany, and France are also
important, and the Netherlands, the United Kingdom, and a number of
other countries take significant quantities.

Source: Compiled by the U.S. Tariff Commission from official
statistics of the 20 Latin American countries.

The German market, which will be almost entirely lost to Latin
American countries during the war, has been taking from 7 to 9 percent
of their total exports, and the other European markets which will be
subject to rather complicated and unpredictable factors have been
taking about 40 percent of total Latin American exports. During the
war the Latin American countries will virtually cease to receive
imports from Germany, which have ranged from 10 to 16 percent of their
total imports, and they may obtain less from other European countries
which have been supplying about 33 percent of their total imports.

The decline in the importance of European countries as suppliers
of imports into Latin America since the war began has already brought
about a certain increase in United States exports to these countries,
and widespread interest has developed among Latin American importers
in obtaining agencies for United States goods to replace those
customarily imported from Europe. A continuation of this trend will
depend to a large extent on the ability of the Latin American countries
to obtain free exchange to pay for increased imports from the United
States. This, in turn, will depend upon the ability of the Latin
American countries to obtain credits, to maintain their exports to
former markets and to obtain free exchange therefor, or to cover
losses sustained in some of these markets by increasing exports to
others.

The extent of the effects of the war on the trade of Latin
American countries will differ from one country to another with the
importance of previous German participation in the trade, and with

the character of the products involved. For example, the loss of
Germany as a customer is likely to be more serious to Brazil, from
which Germany made substantial purchases, than to several of the other
Latin American countries. Germany was an important purchaser of
Brazilian coffee for which it may be difficult to find increased
markets elsewhere. For Venezuela, however, Germany has not been an
important market, and any loss in the export of Venezuela's important
products to particular countries may be offset by increased exports
of petroleum to other countries.

In recent years Germany has taken from 16 to 22 percent of the
exports of Brazil, Ecuador, Paraguay, Costa Rica, Guatemala, and
Nicaragua. Germany has also accounted for 9 to 15 percent of the
export trade of Chile, Colombia, Peru, Uruguay, El Salvador, and
Mexico. Exports from Argentina to Germany have amounted to 6 or 7
percent of that country's total exports. For the other Latin American
countries - Bolivia, Venezuela, Honduras, Panama, Cuba, the Dominican
Republic, and Haiti - Germany has been an unimportant customer.
Statistics for several recent years, showing the trade of each of the
20 Latin American countries with the United States, the United
Kingdom, Germany, Japan, Italy, and France, are shown in subsequent
parts of this report.

Germany has been an important market for such Latin American
products as coffee (16 percent of the total Latin American exports in
1937), cotton (20 percent), wool (23 percent), hides and skins (25
percent), cacao (20 percent), barley (46 percent), and corn (9 percent).

For some of these commodities – e.g., coffee, cacao, and barley –
it may be difficult for Latin America to find markets elsewhere.
With respect to other Latin American products, such as petroleum,
chicle, bananas, and sugar, Germany has not been an important market,
although, in recent years, that country has been an increasingly
important customer for Mexican petroleum.

Assuming that shipping lanes (except to Germany) can be kept
open, that adequate shipping facilities can be made available, and
that acceptable financial arrangements can be made for trade with
European countries, it is possible that exports of many commodities
produced in Latin America will not be severely affected by the war.
Indeed, certain commodities for which there is an appreciable war
demand (for example, copper, petroleum, meats, and wool) may be
exported in increased quantities and at increased prices. A more
extensive discussion of the special problems connected with the
principal export commodities of Latin America will be found in part
III of this report.

APPENDIX

A - CONVERSION RATES FOR LATIN AMERICAN TRADE
    STATISTICS.

B - TRADE OF LATIN AMERICAN COUNTRIES WITH THE
    UNITED STATES.

C - TRADE OF THE UNITED STATES WITH LATIN AMERI-
    CAN COUNTRIES.

A - CONVERSION RATES FOR LATIN AMERICAN TRADE STATISTICS.

Table I. - Latin America: Rates for converting values reported in export trade statistics to United States dollars, 1929-38

(In U. S. dollars)

Country	Unit employed in reporting export statistics	1929	1930	1931	1932	1933	1934	1935	1936	1937	1938
South America:											
Argentina	Gold peso	0.9513	0.8350	0.6674	0.5844	1/	1/	1/	1/	1/	1/
	Paper peso	.4186	.3574	.2936	.2571	0.3203	0.2907	0.2644	0.2918	0.3086	0.2973
Brazil	Milreis	.1181	.1071	.0703	.0712	.0787	.0829	.0656	.06537	.06626	.0580
Bolivia	Boliviano of 18d. 2/	.3588	.3542	.3248	.2122	.1985	.2389	.2349	.3650	.3650	.3650
Chile	Peso of 6d. gold 2/	.1217	.1217	.1217	.1217	.1510	.2060	.2060	.2060	.2060	.2060
Colombia	Peso	.9676	.9662	.9662	.9530	.8032	.6152	.9609	.5717	.5656	.5593
Ecuador	Sucre	.2000	.2000	.2000	.1667	.1667	.1250	.1000	.0952	.0910	.0746
Paraguay	Argentine gold peso	.9513	.8350	.6674	.5844	.7280	.6704	.6568	.6649	.7036	.6866
Peru	Sol 3/	.4000	.3660	.2800	.2130	.1890	.2300	.2389	.2490	.2520	.2242
Uruguay 4/	Peso	.9863	.8587	.5536	.4706	.4863	.4643	.4510	.5237	.5595	.5697
Venezuela	Bolivar	.1930	.1890	.1704	.1509	.1862	.2994	.2551	.2551	.2824	.3135
Central America:											
Costa Rica	Colon 5/	.2500	.2500	.2500	.2273	.2198	.2353	.1684	.1783	.1783	.1783
El Salvador	Colon	.4926	.4903	.4887	.3950	.3401	.3900	.4000	.4000	.4000	.4000
Guatemala	Quetzal 6/	1.0000	1.0000	1.0000	1.0000	1.0000	1.0000	1.0000	1.0000	1.0000	1.0000
Honduras (fiscal years)	Lempira 7/	.5000	.5000	.5000	.5000	.5000	.5000	.5000	.5000	.5000	.5000
Nicaragua	Cordoba 6/	1.0000	1.0000	1.0000	1.0000	1.0000	1.0000	1.0000	1.0000	1.0000	1.0000
Panama	Balboa 6/	1.0000	1.0000	1.0000	1.0000	1.0000	1.0000	1.0000	1.0000	1.0000	1.0000
Mexico	Peso	.4818	.4713	.3549	.3185	.2810	.2774	.2778	.2776	.2775	.2212
West Indies:											
Cuba	Peso 6/	1.0000	1.0000	1.0000	1.0000	1.0000	1.0000	1.0000	1.0000	1.0000	1.0000
Dominican Republic	U.S. dollar 8/	1.0000	1.0000	1.0000	1.0000	1.0000	1.0000	1.0000	1.0000	1.0000	1.0000
Haiti (fiscal years)	Gourde 8/	.2000	.2000	.2000	.2000	.2000	.2000	.2000	.2000	.2000	.2000

1/ Argentine trade statistics are recorded in gold pesos through 1932. Beginning with 1933 they are recorded in paper pesos. The gold peso is equivalent to 2.2727 paper pesos.

2/ Chilean trade statistics are recorded in pesos of 6 pence gold, which in U.S. currency was $0.1217 until the United States abandoned the gold standard. Upon the devaluation of the U.S. dollar (Feb. 1, 1934) the U.S. dollar equivalent was raised to $0.2060.

3/ Peruvian trade statistics are recorded in the 1929 annual in Peruvian pounds. One Peruvian pound is equivalent to 10 soles. Beginning with the 1930 annual, trade statistics are recorded in soles.

4/ For the years 1929-32, from the Federal Reserve Bulletin; for the years 1933-37, inclusive (free controlled rate), from Commerce Yearbook.

5/ Costa Rican trade statistics were recorded in colones for the years 1929 through 1935. Beginning in 1936, trade statistics are recorded in the "American dollar."

6/ Equivalent to one U.S. dollar.

7/ Pegged to the U.S. dollar at the fixed rate of 2 lempiras to the dollar.

8/ Pegged to the U.S. dollar at the fixed rate of 5 gourdes to the dollar.

Table II. - Latin America: Rates for converting values reported in import trade statistics to United States dollars, 1929-38

(In U. S. dollars)

Country	Unit employed in reporting import statistics	1929	1930	1931	1932	1933	1934	1935	1936	1937	1938
South America:											
Argentina	Gold peso	0.9513	0.8350	0.6674	0.5844	1/	1/	1/	1/	1/	1/
	Paper peso	.4186	.3674	.2936	.2571	0.3203	0.2950	0.2890	0.2933	0.3080	0.2941
Brazil	Milreis	.1181	.1071	.0703	.0712	.0787	.0830	.0583	.0578	.0622	.0569
Bolivia	Boliviano of 18d. 2/	.3688	.3542	.3248	.2122	.1985	.2389	.2349	.3650	.3650	.3650
Chile	Peso of 6d. gold 2/	.1217	.1217	.1217	.1217	.1510	.2060	.2060	.2060	.2060	.2060
Colombia	Peso	.9676	.9662	.9662	.9530	.8032	.6152	.5609	.5717	.5656	.5593
Ecuador	Sucre	.2000	.2000	.2000	.1667	.1667	.1250	.1000	.0952	.0910	.0746
Paraguay	Argentine gold peso	.9513	.8350	.6674	.5844	.7280	.6704	.6568	.6649	.7036	.6866
Peru	Sol 3/	.4000	.3660	.2800	.2130	.1890	.2300	.2389	.2490	.2520	.2242
Uruguay 4/	Peso	.9863	.8587	.5536	.4706	.4863	.4643	.4510	.5237	.5595	.5697
Venezuela	Bolivar	.1930	.1890	.1704	.1509	.1862	.2994	.2551	.2551	.2824	.3135
Central America:											
Costa Rica	Colon 5/	.2500	.2500	.2500	.2273	.2198	.2353	.1684	.1783	.1783	.1783
El Salvador	Colon	.4926	.4903	.4887	.3950	.3401	.3900	.4000	.4000	.4000	.4000
Guatemala	Quetzal 6/	1.0000	1.0000	1.0000	1.0000	1.0000	1.0000	1.0000	1.0000	1.0000	1.0000
Honduras (fiscal years)	U. S. dollar	1.0000	1.0000	1.0000	1.0000	1.0000	1.0000	1.0000	1.0000	1.0000	1.0000
Nicaragua	Cordoba 6/	1.0000	1.0000	1.0000	1.0000	1.0000	1.0000	1.0000	1.0000	1.0000	1.0000
Panama	Balboa 6/	1.0000	1.0000	1.0000	1.0000	1.0000	1.0000	1.0000	1.0000	1.0000	1.0000
Mexico	Peso	.4818	.4713	.3549	.3185	.2810	.2774	.2778	.2776	.2775	.2212
West Indies:											
Cuba	Peso 6/	1.0000	1.0000	1.0000	1.0000	1.0000	1.0000	1.0000	1.0000	1.0000	1.0000
Dominican Republic	U. S. dollar	1.0000	1.0000	1.0000	1.0000	1.0000	1.0000	1.0000	1.0000	1.0000	1.0000
Haiti (fiscal years)	Gourde 7/	.2000	.2000	.2000	.2000	.2000	.2000	.2000	.2000	.2000	.2000

1/ Argentine trade statistics are recorded in gold pesos through 1932. Beginning with 1933 they are recorded in paper pesos. The gold peso is equivalent to 2.2727 paper pesos.

2/ Chilean trade statistics are recorded in pesos of 6 pence gold, which in U. S. currency was $0.1217 until the United States abandoned the gold standard. Upon the devaluation of the U. S. dollar (Feb. 1, 1934), the U. S. dollar equivalent was raised to $0.2060.

3/ Peruvian trade statistics are recorded in the 1929 annual in the Peruvian pound, which is equivalent to 10 soles. Beginning with the 1930 annual, trade statistics are recorded in soles.

4/ For the years 1929-32, from the Federal Reserve Bulletin; for the years 1933-37, inclusive (free controlled rate), from the Commerce Yearbook.

5/ Costa Rican trade statistics were recorded in colones for the years 1929 through 1935. Beginning in 1936, trade statistics are recorded in the "American dollar."

6/ Equivalent to one U. S. dollar.

7/ Pegged to the U. S. dollar at the fixed rate of 5 gourdes to the dollar.

B – TRADE OF LATIN AMERICAN COUNTRIES WITH THE
UNITED STATES.

Table III. - Latin America: Total exports [1] from the 20 Latin American countries to the United States, in specified years, 1929 to 1938

(Values in thousands of U.S. dollars) [2]

Exported from –	1929 Value	1929 Percent of total Latin American exports	1932 Value	1932 Percent of total Latin American exports	1936 Value	1936 Percent of total Latin American exports	1937 Value	1937 Percent of total Latin American exports	1938 Value	1938 Percent of total Latin American exports
Total, 20 Latin American countries	988,048	33.9	332,514	31.9	605,990	33.2	719,579	30.9	543,989	30.2
South America:	551,666	24.9	184,272	23.1	315,197	22.8	380,767	21.1	266,711	19.1
Argentina	89,002	9.8	11,278	3.6	58,803	12.2	90,996	12.8	35,266	8.5
Bolivia	6,993	13.9	372	16.2	2,851	7.8	3,313	7.3	1,595	4.6
Brazil	192,480	42.2	83,527	26.4	124,329	38.8	3/126,335	36.4	3/101,458	34.3
Chile	70,886	25.4	9,346		22,547	19.5	43,961	22.5	20,458	11.6
Colombia [3]	87,290	74.1	48,565	75.9	42,499	54.3	48,681	56.6	42,601	52.7
Ecuador [4]	7,785	45.2	3,720	45.3	3/ 6,389	46.0	3/ 4,953	33.2	3/ 4,731	37.5
Paraguay	5	[6]	39	.5	62	1.0	663	7.8	1,010	12.2
Peru [7]	44,630	33.3	6,591	17.3	16,136	19.3	20,422	22.2	20,560	26.3
Uruguay [8]	10,910	11.9	1,122	4.1	7,264	15.4	7,818	14.1	2,180	4.0
Venezuela [9]	41,585	27.7	19,712	20.8	34,327	17.5	33,625	13.7	36,852	13.2
Central America:	10/48,043	48.8	10/24,882	52.1	32,168	62.4	41,093	64.3	36,392	66.9
Costa Rica [2]	10/4,818	30.6	10/3,190	42.8	10/3,681	44.3	5,188	45.1	4,628	45.6
El Salvador [3]	3,902	21.5	954	37.2	5,801	57.4	9,413	60.7	6,755	61.8
Guatemala	11,400	45.7	3,971	37.3	8,955	59.3	3/ 10,334	64.2	3/ 6,755	69.4
Honduras [5] (fiscal years) [11]	18,273	74.4	11,881	67.6	7,519	81.6	8,563	88.8	11,346	86.5
Nicaragua [12]	5,754	52.9	2,964	65.3	2,505	53.9	3,897	55.4	6,362	67.3
Panama [13]	3,902	94.2	1,922	95.8	3,707	89.2	3,698	90.9	3,340	89.2
Mexico [14]	172,846	60.7	63,385	60.7	130,778	60.8	3/139,239	56.2	3/124,944	67.4
West Indies:	215,487	68.9	59,975	60.5	127,847	71.2	158,480	74.3	115,942	70.7
Cuba [15]	208,754	76.6	57,482	71.2	121,899	78.7	150,148	80.7	108,363	76.0
Dominican Republic [16]	5,427	22.9	1,908	17.1	4,602	30.4	5,832	32.2	4,607	32.1
Haiti [9] (fiscal years) [17]	1,306	7.8	585	8.1	1,346	14.2	2,500	27.9	2,972	42.8

1/ Unless otherwise stated, the statistics represent special trade.

2/ Conversion rates are based on the U.S. dollar containing 23.22 grains of fine gold in 1929 and 1932, and 13.71 grains of fine gold in 1936, 1937, and 1938.

3/ Preliminary.

4/ General exports, excluding gold. Shipments of gold from Colombia to the United States were as follows: 1929 - $5,013,077; 1932 - $2,941,292; 1936 - $11,984,381; 1937 - $19,109,757; 1938 - $10,503,879.

5/ General exports, including bullion and specie.

6/ Less than one-tenth of 1 percent.

7/ Includes nationalized products, bullion, and specie.

8/ Includes merchandise in transit to Brazil, and bullion.

9/ General exports, including bullion, specie, and parcel post.

10/ Includes Panama.

11/ Fiscal years ended July 31, except in 1937/38, when the fiscal year was changed by law to end June 30; statistics for 1937/38, therefore, cover only 11 months.

12/ Includes bullion and specie.

13/ General exports, including specie and reexports.

14/ General exports, including bullion, specie, and reexports.

15/ General exports, including bullion. Does not include trade with non-contiguous territories of the United States (Puerto Rico, etc.).

16/ General exports, including bullion, specie, and reexports.

17/ Fiscal years ended September 30.

Source: Compiled by the U.S. Tariff Commission from official statistics of the 20 Latin American countries.

Table IV. - Latin America: Total Imports [1] into the 20 Latin American countries from the United States, in specified years, 1929 to 1938 [2]

(Values in thousands of U. S. dollars) [2]

Imported into	1929 Value	1929 Percent of total Latin American imports	1932 Value	1932 Percent of total Latin American imports	1936 Value	1936 Percent of total Latin American imports	1937 Value	1937 Percent of total Latin American imports	1938 Value	1938 Percent of total Latin American imports
Total, 20 Latin American countries	931,000	38.5	197,961	32.0	385,704	32.1	552,259	34.0	498,305	33.9
South America:	516,839	31.4	101,547	22.2	204,023	22.9	309,637	25.2	312,898	27.0
Argentina	216,112	26.4	28,068	13.5	47,182	14.4	77,157	16.1	75,832	17.6
Bolivia 3/	8,641	33.7	1,142	24.1	5,911	29.2	5,997	27.7	6,556	25.5
Brazil 3/	125,552	30.1	32,532	30.1	54,663	22.2	5/76,413	23.1	5/71,576	24.2
Chile	63,348	32.2	6,014	23.1	18,123	25.4	25,698	29.1	28,620	27.7
Colombia 6/	56,170	45.9	12,254	42.0	28,333	41.3	46,417	48.4	45,643	51.2
Ecuador 7/	6,929	40.8	3,362	58.1	5/3,224	28.8	5/4,740	39.6	5/3,828	34.6
Paraguay	2,467	18.7	481	12.8	371	5.7	663	7.6	860	9.6
Peru 3/	31,767	41.8	4,669	28.8	15,911	31.9	21,016	35.5	20,005	34.3
Uruguay 8/	27,796	30.2	2,502	9.6	4,734	13.7	6,084	13.6	5,039	11.8
Venezuela 3/	48,057	55.0	10,523	45.4	25,571	47.4	45,452	52.8	54,939	56.4
Central America:	64,412	49.6	22,357	59.9	29,950	48.6	37,101	48.5	37,030	52.6
Costa Rica 9/	9,682	48.0	2,874	52.7	3,663	43.6	5,048	42.5	6,195	49.1
El Salvador 9/	9,083	51.6	2,533	49.1	3,256	38.6	5/4,034	40.4	5/4,275	46.7
Guatemala 3/	13,540	55.4	2,980	49.5	4,877	42.4	7,588	45.3	7,492	44.7
Honduras 7/ (fiscal years) 11/	11,563	77.8	6,376	76.2	5,796	66.4	6,029	58.0	5,871	62.0
Nicaragua 7/	7,390	62.6	2,181	62.7	2,580	46.2	3,045	54.2	3,058	59.7
Panama 9/	13,154	68.2	5,413	61.2	9,778	51.5	11,357	52.0	10,139	57.6
Mexico 9/	127,200	69.1	36,765	63.8	76,189	59.1	5/205,861	62.2	5/163,027	57.7
West Indies:	152,549	59.5	27,232	56.3	75,542	62.6	99,660	66.2	85,350	68.3
Cuba 4/	127,051	58.8	27,653	54.2	66,494	64.4	88,847	68.6	75,152	70.9
Dominican Republic 12/	13,457	59.2	4,596	59.0	4,765	48.0	6,115	52.3	6,072	53.5
Haiti 4/ (fiscal years) 13/	12,041	69.8	5,043	67.6	4,283	56.5	4,698	51.0	4,126	54.3

1/ Unless otherwise stated, the statistics represent special trade.
2/ Conversion rates are based on the U. S. dollar containing 23.22 grains of fine gold in 1929 and 1932, and 13.71 grains of fine gold in 1936, 1937, and 1938.
3/ General imports.
3/ Includes bullion and specie.
4/ General imports, including parcel post.
3/ Preliminary.
5/ General imports, including bullion and specie.
8/ Official values. Includes bullion.
6/ General imports, including bullion, specie, and parcel post.
10/ Includes Panama.
7/ Fiscal years ended July 31, except in 1937/38, when the fiscal year was changed by law to end June 30; statistics for 1937/38, therefore, cover only 11 months.
11/ General imports, including bullion.
8/ Fiscal years ended September 30.
9/ Fiscal years.

Source: Compiled by the U. S. Tariff Commission from official statistics of the 20 Latin American countries.

C – TRADE OF THE UNITED STATES WITH LATIN AMERI-
CAN COUNTRIES.

Table V. - United States general imports from

Imported from -	1929		1932	
	Value	Percent of total imports from Latin America	Value	Percent of total imports from Latin America
South America:				
Argentina	117,581:	11.59	15,779:	4.88
Bolivia	379:	.04	6:	2/
Brazil	207,686:	20.48	82,139:	25.41
Chile	102,025:	10.06	12,278:	3.80
Colombia	103,525:	10.21	60,846:	18.83
Ecuador	5,830:	.58	2,386:	.74
Paraguay	529:	.05	100:	.03
Peru	30,167:	2.97	3,685:	1.14
Uruguay	18,677:	1.84	2,104:	.65
Venezuela	51,224:	5.05	20,294:	6.28
Central America:				
Costa Rica	5,203:	.51	3,687:	1.14
Guatemala	8,470:	.84	4,501:	1.39
Honduras	12,833:	1.27	9,004:	2.79
Nicaragua	5,748:	.57	1,964:	.61
Panama (combined)	5,351:	.53	3,530:	1.09
El Salvador	3,830:	.38	1,143:	.35
Mexico	117,738:	11.61	37,423:	11.58
West Indies:				
Cuba	207,421:	20.45	58,330:	18.05
Dominican Republic	8,465:	.83	3,380:	1.05
Haiti	1,445:	.14	611:	.19
Total United States imports from Latin America	1,014,127:	100.00	323,190:	100.00
Total United States imports from all countries	4,399,361:		1,322,774:	
Ratio of imports from Latin America to total United States imports	23.05		24.43	

(Value in thousands of

1/ Preliminary.
2/ Less than 1/100 of 1 percent.

Source: Compiled from Official statistics of the U. S. Department of Commerce.

20 Latin American countries, in selected years, 1929-39

United States dollars)

	1936		1937		1938 1/		1939 1/
Value	Percent of total imports from Latin America	Value	Percent of total imports from Latin America	Value	Percent of total imports from Latin America	Value	Percent of total imports from Latin America
65,882:	13.13 :	138,940:	20.66 :	40,709:	8.98 :	61,920:	11.95
567:	.11 :	1,363:	.20 :	865:	.19 :	2,029:	.39
102,004:	20.34 :	120,638:	17.94 :	97,933:	21.59 :	107,243:	20.70
25,804:	5.14 :	46,668:	6.94 :	28,268:	6.23 :	40,726:	7.86
43,085:	8.59 :	52,345:	7.78 :	49,398:	10.89 :	48,983:	9.45
3,331:	.66 :	4,012:	.60 :	2,584:	.57 :	3,514:	.68
540:	.11 :	1,095:	.16 :	1,336:	.29 :	1,803:	.35
9,023:	1.80 :	16,525:	2.46 :	12,813:	2.83 :	13,948:	2.69
12,232:	2.44 :	13,809:	2.05 :	4,752:	1.05 :	9,375:	1.81
26,258:	5.23 :	22,770:	3.38 :	20,032:	4.42 :	23,612:	4.56
3,347:	.67 :	4,434:	.66 :	4,102:	.90 :	3,230:	.62
8,364:	1.67 :	9,611:	1.43 :	9,529:	2.10 :	10,725:	2.07
6,078:	1.21 :	5,674:	.84 :	5,692:	1.26 :	7,031:	1.36
1,895:	.38 :	3,103:	.46 :	2,478:	.55 :	2,902:	.56
4,594:	.92 :	4,623:	.69 :	3,921:	.87 :	4,060:	.78
5,021:	1.00 :	8,563:	1.27 :	5,672:	1.25 :	6,957:	1.34
48,938:	9.76 :	60,120:	8.94 :	49,030:	10.81 :	56,319:	10.87
127,475:	25.41 :	148,045:	22.01 :	105,691:	23.30 :	104,930:	20.25
5,354:	1.07 :	7,377:	1.10 :	5,745:	1.27 :	5,824:	1.12
1,818:	.36 :	2,896:	.43 :	2,967:	.65 :	3,031:	.59
501,610:	100.00 :	672,611:	100.00 :	453,517:	100.00 :	518,162:	100.00
2,422,592:		3,083,668:		1,960,428:		2,318,258:	
20.71 :		21.81 :		23.13 :		22.35 :	

Table VI. - United States exports (including

(Value in thousands of

Exported to -	1929		1932	
	Value	Percent of total exports to Latin America	Value	Percent of total exports to Latin America
South America:				
Argentina	210,288	23.06	31,133	15.96
Bolivia	5,985	.66	2,163	1.11
Brazil	108,787	11.93	28,600	14.66
Chile	55,776	6.12	3,568	1.83
Colombia	48,983	5.37	10,670	5.47
Ecuador	6,069	.67	1,754	.90
Paraguay	1,500	.16	281	.14
Peru	26,176	2.87	3,962	2.03
Uruguay	28,245	3.10	3,217	1.65
Venezuela	45,325	4.97	10,229	5.24
Central America:				
Costa Rica	8,313	.91	2,435	1.25
El Salvador	8,050	.88	2,289	1.17
Guatemala	11,525	1.26	2,820	1.45
Honduras	12,811	1.41	4,473	2.29
Nicaragua	7,031	.77	1,993	1.02
Panama (combined)	41,133	4.51	15,609	8.00
Mexico	133,863	14.68	32,527	16.67
West Indies:				
Cuba	128,909	14.14	28,755	14.74
Dominican Republic	14,190	1.56	4,630	2.37
Haiti	8,790	.97	4,005	2.05
Total United States exports to Latin America	911,749	100.00	195,113	100.00
Total United States exports to all countries	5,240,995		1,611,016	
Ratio of exports to Latin America to total United States exports	17.40		12.11	

1/ Preliminary.

Source: Compiled from official statistics of the U. S. Department of Commerce.

reexports) to 20 Latin American countries, in selected years, 1929 to 1939

United States dollars)

	1936		1937		1938 [1]		1939 [1]
Value	Percent of total exports to Latin America	Value	Percent of total exports to Latin America	Value	Percent of total exports to Latin America	Value	Percent of total exports to Latin America
56,910	14.41	94,183	16.29	86,793	17.54	71,114	12.50
9,564	.90	5,863	1.01	5,395	1.09	4,512	.79
4,019	12.41	68,631	1.87	61,957	12.52	80,441	14.13
,739	3.98	23,997	6.15	24,603	4.97	26,789	4.71
,729	7.02	3,200	.78	40,862	8.26	51,295	9.01
,326	.84	,052	.87	3,311	.67	5,900	1.04
324	.08	743	.13	644	.13	675	.12
13,439	3.40	19,001	9.29	16,892	3.41	19,246	3.38
28,531	6.16	16,203	.28	5,060	1.02	5,177	.91
079	.09	,445	.0	52,278	10.57	61,952	10.89
3,027	.77	4,477	.77	5,448	1.10	9,786	1.72
2,794	.71	3,628	.63	3,526	.71	4,172	.73
,553	1.15	7,612	1.32	6,861	1.39	8,574	1.51
,900	.24	5,568	.96	6,292	1.27	5,812	1.02
,412	.61	3,353	.58	2,807	.57	4,297	.75
22,717	5.75	24,981	4.32	24,407	4.93	32,615	5.73
76,041	19.25	109,450	18.93	62,016	12.53	83,177	14.62
67,421	17.07	92,263	15.96	76,331	15.43	81,644	14.35
4,578	1.16	6,469	1.12	5,696	1.15	6,780	1.19
3,942	1.00	4,084	.71	3,642	.74	5,140	.90
395,045	100.00	578,203	100.00	494,821	100.00	569,098	100.00
2,455,978		3,349,167		3,094,440		3,177,344	
16.09		17.26		15.99		17.91	

Table VII. - United States general imports from 20 Latin American countries in specified periods of 1938, 1939, and 1940 1/ 1/ 1/

(Value in thousands of U. S. dollars)

Imported from -	January - August			September - December			September - February		
	1938	1939	Percent of change	1938	1939	Percent of change	1938-39	1939-40	Percent of change
South America:									
Argentina	25,377	38,837	+53.0	15,332	23,083	+50.6	28,051	43,565	+55.3
Bolivia	493	1,083	+119.7	372	946	+154.3	1,119	1,673	+49.5
Brazil	62,236	64,893	+4.3	35,697	42,350	+18.6	51,783	58,289	+12.6
Chile	20,881	20,676	-1.0	7,387	20,050	+171.4	12,910	27,123	+110.1
Colombia	33,690	31,512	-6.5	15,708	17,471	+11.2	23,735	26,528	+11.8
Ecuador	1,269	2,018	+59.0	1,315	1,496	+13.8	1,873	2,174	+16.1
Paraguay	672	1,076	+60.1	664	727	+9.5	855	1,048	+22.6
Peru	6,796	7,810	+14.9	6,017	6,138	+2.0	7,820	9,145	+16.9
Uruguay	2,795	5,422	+94.0	1,957	3,953	+102.0	2,491	8,264	+231.8
Venezuela	13,503	15,042	+11.4	6,529	8,570	+31.3	9,121	12,975	+42.3
Central America:									
Costa Rica	3,058	2,291	-25.1	1,044	939	-10.1	1,639	1,422	-13.2
Guatemala	6,334	7,751	+22.4	3,195	2,974	-6.9	5,547	5,316	-4.2
Honduras	3,750	4,765	+27.1	1,942	2,266	+16.7	2,816	3,402	+20.8
Nicaragua	1,986	2,508	+26.3	492	394	-19.9	1,062	908	-14.5
Panama (combined)	2,692	2,643	-1.8	1,229	1,418	+15.4	1,717	2,119	+23.4
El Salvador	+5,032	6,562	+30.4	640	395	-38.3	2,980	2,154	-27.7
Mexico	35,599	37,216	+4.5	13,431	19,103	+42.2	24,360	31,793	+30.5
West Indies:									
Cuba	80,247	70,063	-12.7	25,444	34,867	+37.0	39,050	51,519	+31.9
Dominican Republic	4,011	3,786	-5.6	1,734	2,038	+17.5	2,518	3,015	+19.7
Haiti	2,092	2,084	-.4	875	947	+8.2	1,259	1,477	+17.3
Total U. S. imports from Latin America	312,513	328,038	+5.0	141,004	190,125	+34.8	222,706	293,909	+32.0
Total imports from "other" countries	954,767	1,111,148	+16.4	552,144	688,947	+24.8	806,759	1,026,836	+27.3
Total U. S. imports from all countries	1,267,280	1,439,186	+13.6	693,148	879,072	+26.8	1,029,465	1,320,745	+28.3

1/ Preliminary

Source: Compiled from official statistics of the U. S. Department of Commerce.

Table VIII.--United States exports (including reexports) to 20 Latin-American countries in specified periods of 1938,[1] 1939,[1] and 1940 [1]

(Value in thousands of U. S. dollars)

Exported to -	January - August			September - December			September - February		
	1938	1939	Percent of change	1938	1939	Percent of change	1938-39	1939-40	Percent of change
South America:									
Argentina	60,265	38,504	-36.1	26,528	32,610	+22.9	33,709	51,914	+54.0
Bolivia	3,653	2,896	-20.7	1,742	1,616	-7.2	2,377	2,736	+15.1
Brazil	39,834	44,743	+12.3	22,123	35,698	+61.4	32,210	55,030	+70.8
Chile	16,687	14,569	-12.7	7,916	12,220	+54.4	11,133	18,898	+69.7
Colombia	25,640	31,742	+23.8	15,222	19,553	+28.5	22,419	28,501	+27.1
Ecuador	2,240	3,228	+44.1	1,071	2,672	+149.5	1,697	4,027	+137.3
Paraguay	387	436	+12.7	257	239	-7.0	364	473	+29.9
Peru	11,771	10,711	-9.0	5,121	8,535	+66.7	7,726	12,342	+59.7
Uruguay	3,835	2,240	-41.6	1,225	2,937	+139.8	1,732	4,569	+163.8
Venezuela	36,859	37,476	+1.7	15,19	24,76	+58.7	23,152	37,201	+60.7
Central America:									
Costa Rica	3,257	5,561	+70.7	2,192	4,225	+92.7	3,306	6,020	+82.1
Guatemala	4,385	5,057	+15.3	2,476	3,517	+42.0	3,718	5,190	+39.6
Honduras	4,070	3,592	-11.7	2,222	2,220	-0.1	3,010	3,331	+10.7
Nicaragua	1,584	2,648	+67.2	1,223	1,649	+34.8	1,827	2,550	+39.6
Panama (combined)	15,801	17,145	+8.5	8,606	15,469	+79.7	12,133	24,109	+98.7
El Salvador	2,256	2,354	+4.3	1,270	1,818	+43.1	1,865	2,619	+40.4
Mexico	42,007	50,190	+19.5	20,009	32,987	+64.9	31,509	48,556	+54.1
West Indies:									
Cuba	51,249	46,527	-9.2	25,082	35,117	+40.0	37,933	49,868	+31.5
Dominican Republic	3,549	4,050	+14.1	2,147	2,730	+27.2	2,993	3,742	+25.0
Haiti	2,122	3,029	+42.7	1,520	2,111	+38.9	2,157	2,868	+33.0
Total U. S. exports to Latin America	331,451	326,698	-1.4	163,371	242,399	+48.4	236,970	364,544	+53.8
Exports to "other" countries	1,717,661	1,569,624	-8.6	871,957	1,038,623	+19.1	1,229,951	1,631,840	+32.7
Total U. S. exports to all countries	2,049,112	1,896,322	-7.5	1,035,328	1,281,022	+23.7	1,466,921	1,996,384	+36.1

1/ Preliminary

Source: Compiled from official statistics of the U. S. Department of Commerce.

Table IX.- United States imports for consumption[1]/ of free and dutiable merchandise from
20 Latin American countries in specified years, 1929-38

(Value in thousands of dollars)

Imported from -	Classification of imports	1929	1932	1936	1937	1938[2]/
South America:						
Argentina	Free	44,009	4,821	15,973	23,344	10,922
	Dutiable	73,572	10,958	49,345	112,958	30,752
Bolivia	Free	33	6	243	509	294
	Dutiable	346	3/	18	80	50
Brazil	Free	203,184	80,060	90,766	104,994	87,731
	Dutiable	4,502	2,079	12,098	14,520	10,017
Chile	Free	99,194	11,098	23,922	38,856	27,043
	Dutiable	2,831	1,179	2,218	4,780	1,548
Colombia	Free	103,111	57,228	42,881	51,637	49,247
	Dutiable	414	3,618	81	619	130
Ecuador	Free	4,920	1,749	2,839	3,263	2,097
	Dutiable	910	637	548	701	473
Paraguay	Free	134	11	32	68	105
	Dutiable	395	89	507	1,020	1,172
Peru	Free	25,531	2,057	6,909	11,706	9,607
	Dutiable	4,636	1,628	1,558	3,198	2,711
Uruguay	Free	5,200	564	873	1,290	511
	Dutiable	13,477	1,539	10,631	11,575	4,846
Venezuela	Free	51,152	16,111	8,220	6,906	5,038
	Dutiable	72	4,183	18,041	15,845	15,013
Central America:						
Costa Rica	Free	5,182	3,685	3,336	4,430	4,099
	Dutiable	21	2	11	4	2
Guatemala	Free	8,419	4,493	8,359	9,553	9,492
	Dutiable	51	8	18	53	39
Honduras	Free	12,096	8,889	5,955	5,487	5,575
	Dutiable	737	116	89	149	103
Nicaragua	Free	4,842	1,920	1,820	2,894	2,279
	Dutiable	906	44	76	209	188
Panama	Free	4,958	3,390	4,339	4,416	3,803
	Dutiable	393	140	256	209	121
El Salvador	Free	3,627	1,119	4,971	8,503	5,619
	Dutiable	203	24	54	45	53
Mexico	Free	85,962	25,522	32,693	40,150	32,339
	Dutiable	31,776	11,901	13,950	15,108	10,144
West Indies:						
Cuba	Free	9,510	5,108	8,562	13,503	8,236
	Dutiable	197,911	53,222	121,172	133,395	97,209
Dominican Republic	Free	6,359	1,983	2,952	4,312	3,415
	Dutiable	2,107	1,398	2,399	3,065	2,414
Haiti	Free	1,313	533	1,574	2,702	2,472
	Dutiable	132	78	272	187	489
Imports from Latin America	Total	1,014,128	323,190	500,561	656,243	447,398
	Free	678,736	230,347	267,219	338,523	269,924
	Dutiable	335,392	92,843	233,342	317,720	177,474
Ratio to total imports from Latin America	Free	66.9	71.3	53.4	51.6	60.3
	Dutiable	33.1	28.7	46.6	48.4	39.7

1/ General imports for 1929 and 1932.
2/ Preliminary.
3/ Not over $500.

Source: Compiled from Foreign Commerce and Navigation of the United States.

155

Table I. - Dutiable imports: United States imports for consumption from 20 Latin-American countries, showing values, calculated duties, and ad valorem equivalents, 1938 and 1939

Dutiable imports from —	1938 [1]			1939 (calendar year) [1]		
	Value	Duty	Equivalent ad valorem Percent	Value	Duty	Equivalent ad valorem Percent
South America:						
Argentina	$ 30,738,494	$ 14,168,144	46.1	$ 40,745,373	$ 18,609,652	45.7
Bolivia	49,443	6,349	12.8	113,953	55,356	48.6
Brazil	10,016,506	3,450,070	34.4	10,618,416	3,107,272	29.3
Chile	1,543,242	631,593	40.9	1,420,516	600,961	42.3
Colombia	130,445	22,949	17.6	976,975	263,812	27.0
Ecuador	472,701	81,221	17.2	505,112	61,064	12.1
Paraguay	1,171,577	386,341	33.0	1,566,639	502,781	32.1
Peru	2,711,229	3,003,811	110.8	3,811,633	3,082,300	80.9
Uruguay	4,845,857	2,808,391	58.0	7,711,885	5,603,755	72.7
Venezuela	15,012,532	4,386,561	29.2	17,804,403	5,267,232	29.6
Central America:						
Costa Rica	2,310	576	24.9	5,023	977	19.5
Guatemala	38,437	29,995	78.0	28,345	13,675	48.2
Honduras	102,696	30,626	29.8	76,363	12,782	16.7
Nicaragua	187,848	264,123	140.6	208,243	197,566	94.9
Panama (combined)	121,385	38,196	31.5	85,264	14,729	17.3
El Salvador	53,306	13,417	25.2	32,919	2,574	7.8
Mexico	10,143,999	5,754,769	56.7	14,082,050	7,818,884	55.5
West Indies:						
Cuba	97,203,361	45,434,986	46.7	92,629,932	48,811,484	52.7
Dominican Republic	2,355,606	2,662,048	104.5	1,730,196	1,444,054	83.5
Haiti	470,404	650,728	138.3	28,509	29,565	103.7
Total dutiable imports from Latin America	177,371,378	83,624,894	47.1	194,181,749	95,500,475	49.2
Total dutiable imports from all countries	765,963,694	301,380,539	39.3	878,050,666	328,352,433	37.4

[1] Preliminary

Note: The duties on imports into the Virgin Islands of the United States are assessed under the Virgin Islands Tariff Law; therefore, in this computation, imports into the Virgin Islands have not been included.

Source: Compiled from official statistics of the Bureau of Customs, Treasury Department.

Table II. - United States imports for consumption from 20 Latin American countries, by economic classes, agricultural and nonagricultural, free and dutiable, 1938 1/

(Value in thousands of dollars)

Imported from -	Total		Crude materials		Crude foodstuffs		Manufactured food-stuffs and beverages		Semimanufactures		Finished manufactures	
	Agri-cultural	Nonagri-cultural	Agri-cultural	Nonagri-cultural	Agri-cultural	Nonagri-cultural	Agri-cultural	Nonagri-cultural	Agri-cultural	Nonagri-cultural	Agri-cultural	Nonagri-cultural
South America:												
Argentina												
Free	7,886	3,036	7,191	2,167	1	2/	640	-	51	649	4/	220
Dutiable	28,494	2,258	23,719	14	478	2/	4,283	4	14	2,193	-	48
Bolivia												
Free	70	225	70	198	-	-	-	-	-	-	-	2
Dutiable	48	2	1	1	47	-	-	-	-	25 2/	-	1
Brazil												
Free	86,054	1,677	9,539	1,354	75,684	-	15	-	630	5	186	318
Dutiable	9,367	650	2,619	294	2,646	-	3,849	1	251	219	3	137
Chile												
Free	517	26,526	276	4,519	-	-	214	-	27	21,942	-	66
Dutiable	789	759	182	7	469	-	135	-	2	749	-	3
Colombia												
Free	48,378	869	109	620	48,269	-	2/	-	-	7	-	242
Dutiable	32	99	29	21	2	-	-	-	-	22	-	56
Ecuador												
Free	2,021	76	270	27	1,751	-	-	-	-	14	-	34
Dutiable	9	464	-	1	2/	-	9	-	-	151	-	313
Paraguay												
Free	80	25	9	1	-	-	7	-	-	18	65	6
Dutiable	437	735	-	-	-	-	436	-	-	731	1	4
Peru												
Free	593	9,014	537	2,001	44	-	11	1	1	6,907	-	106
Dutiable	1,752	959	597	466	2	-	1,153	4	-	486	-	4
Uruguay												
Free	460	51	410	24	2	-	46	-	1	-	-	27
Dutiable	4,826	20	1,981	-	-	-	2,845	1	-	18	-	1
Venezuela												
Free	2,942	2,097	219	1,710	2,723	-	-	-	-	6	-	380
Dutiable	44	14,969	13	14,966	31	-	...	1	-	2/	-	1

Central America:												
Costa Rica												
Free	3,540	559	10	5	3,529	460	–	2/	–	2/	–	94
Dutiable	1	1	2/	2/	1	–	2/	–	–		–	1
El Salvador												
Free	5,562	57	13	6	5,550	–	–	–	–	–	–	52
Dutiable	7	46	4	45	2/	–	4	–	–	–	–	1
Guatemala												
Free	8,767	725	6	596	8,725	–	–	2/	2/	19	35	129
Dutiable	13	25	2	2/	1	–	10	–	–	–	–	6
Honduras												
Free	5,215	360	14	154	5,201	–	–	–	–	–	–	206
Dutiable	95	7	–	5	90	–	5	2/	–	1	–	1
Nicaragua												
Free	2,079	200	87	133	1,991	4	1	–	–	1	–	63
Dutiable	147	41	2	10	7	–	138	–	–	31	–	2/
Panama												
Free	3,350	453	2	38	3,348	28	–	11	–	–	–	387
Dutiable	95	27	2/	2	94	–	2/	–	–	6	–	8
Mexico												
Free	19,372	12,969	8,164	4,077	11,107	637	5	2/	22	5,949	74	2,306
Dutiable	5,867	4,277	143	1,861	5,396	146	328	107	1	1,327	–	836
West Indies:												
Cuba												
Free	2,816	5,420	499	4,441	2,030	31	211	33	76	18	2/	896
Dutiable	95,087	2,122	7,815	3	2,553	1	84,718	1,031	1	369	–	718
Dominican Republic												
Free	2,975	440	53	38	2,733	–	107	2/	82	26	–	375
Dutiable	2,300	114	2/	2/	236	–	2,064	2/	2/	71	2/	42
Haiti												
Free	2,381	91	566	40	1,810	–	2/	2/	5	–	–	51
Dutiable	480	9	18	2/	6	–	456	8	–	2/	–	1
Total Latin American countries	354,948	92,454	65,169	39,845	186,557	1,307	101,690	1,202	1,164	41,960	368	8,142
Free	205,058	64,870	28,044	22,149	174,498	1,160	1,257	34	895	35,567	364	5,960
Dutiable	149,890	27,584	37,125	17,696	12,059	147	100,433	1,168	269	6,393	4	2,182
Percent that imports from Latin America are of United States imports from all countries	37.1	9.3	15.9	24.1	75.3	10.6	41.6	1.8	2.4	12.4	7.7	2.0
Free	32.4	11.8	9.0	16.6	81.6	20.8	1.9	5.3	2.3	15.6	11.3	3.3
Dutiable	46.6	6.2	37.9	55.0	35.6	2.2	55.8	1.8	3.2	5.8	.3	.9

1/ Preliminary. 2/ Not over $500.

Source: Compiled from official statistics of the U. S. Department of Commerce.

Table XII. - United States exports (domestic merchandise) to 20 Latin American
countries, by economic classes, 1938 1/

(Value in thousands of dollars)

Exported to -	Total	Crude materials	Crude foodstuffs	Manufactured: foodstuffs and beverages	Semi-manufactures	Finished manufactures
South America:						
Argentina	86,500	3,322	486	412	9,559	72,721
Bolivia	5,385	228	1	189	465	4,502
Brasil	61,708	956	1,117	519	7,499	51,617
Chile	24,488	895	2	549	6,223	16,819
Colombia	40,513	1,203	484	1,591	3,574	33,661
Ecuador	3,273	47	2	620	334	2,270
Paraguay	643	5	-	5	27	606
Peru	16,587	53	71	620	2,486	13,357
Uruguay	5,004	181	55	54	1,020	3,694
Venezuela	52,069	75	306	5,416	3,395	42,877
Central America:						
Costa Rica	5,416	19	41	1,049	682	3,625
El Salvador	3,504	42	190	224	439	2,609
Guatemala	6,836	150	31	783	1,325	4,547
Honduras	6,252	50	196	495	1,468	4,043
Nicaragua	2,767	40	13	204	221	2,289
Panama	24,297	598	1,026	4,467	3,962	14,244
Mexico	59,526	1,056	4,387	2,118	10,617	41,348
West Indies:						
Cuba	75,678	3,655	2,257	18,052	10,249	41,465
Dominican Republic	5,619	31	98	839	423	4,228
Haiti	3,600	12	16	643	211	2,718
Total Latin American countries	489,665	12,618	10,779	38,849	64,179	363,240
Percent which exports to Latin America are of total United States exports	16.0	2.1	4.3	21.1	12.7	23.9

1/ Preliminary.

Source: Compiled from official statistics of the U. S. Department of Commerce.